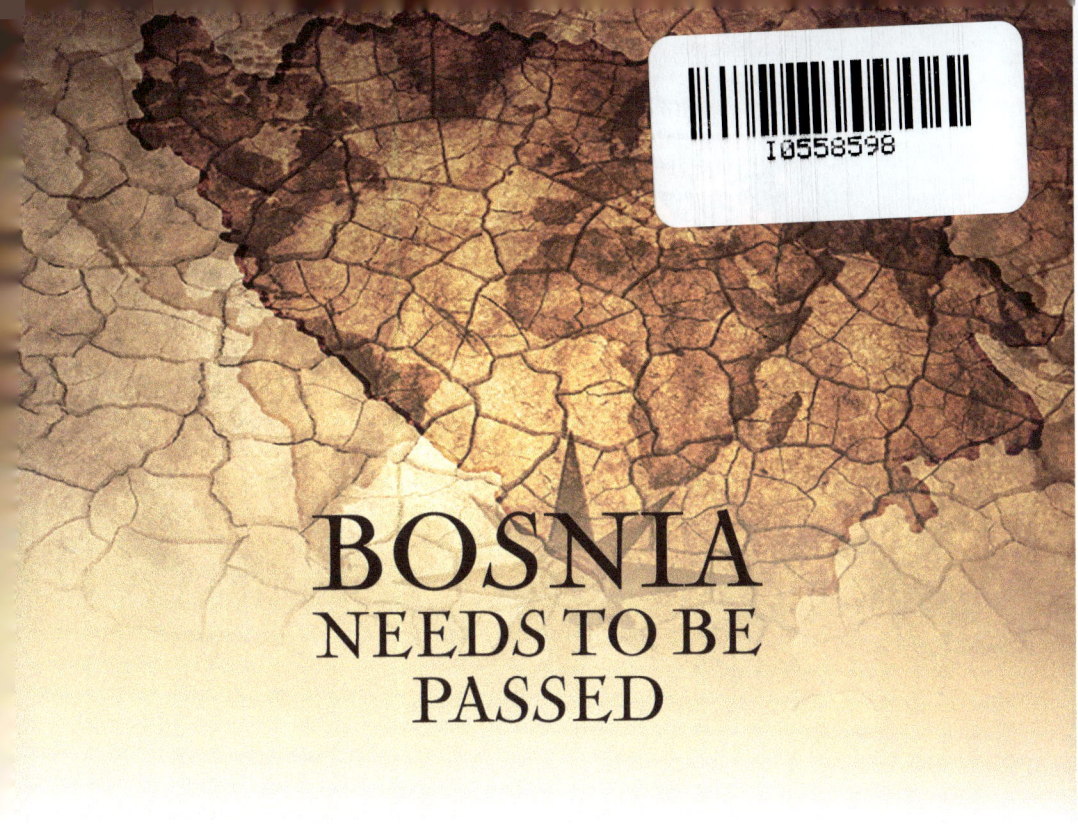

BOSNIA
NEEDS TO BE
PASSED

BOSNIA
NEEDS TO BE
PASSED
Aporias of Elijah of Thunder

Zeljko Vujovic

ARPress
ILLUMINATING IDEAS,
EMPOWERING VOICES

ARPress
45 Dan Road Suite 5
Canton MA 02021

Hotline: 1(888) 821-0229
Fax: 1(508) 545-7580

Ordering Information:

Quantity sales. Special discounts are available on quantity purchases by corporations, associations, and others. For details, contact the publisher at the address above.

Printed in the United States of America.

ISBN-13:   Paperback   979-8-89330-679-8
                eBook   979-8-89330-678-1

Library of Congress Control Number: 2024901783

THE CONTENT

Gratitude to Tamara A. Čapelj, a poet from Sarajevo.

*How do different,
learned people talk about the
common past, present, and future
of living in the Balkans?*

APORIAS[1] OF ELIJAH OF THUNDER

My problem is that I have to go to Vienna, Paris, and London, and the trip is expensive... Airline ticket Podgorica - Vienna, return, low cost, 167-240 euros, Podgorica - Paris, return, low cost, 360-450 euros, Podgorica - London, return, low cost, 260-452 euros ... And the cost of living? America is far away...

They tell me from Bosnia that the Montenegrins got away with it, without punishment, for their criminals. The most important thing, if you already describe all the wars, describe the war in BiH as the aggression of Serbia with Montenegro, and that, with that war, a terrible genocide was committed against Muslims. It is important that the whole world knows and that it is written, that they come and pay their respects at so many cemeteries of the slain. I do not want the daily rhetoric of the aggressors in BiH to be heard.

From Bosnia, what they tell me is the cause of my aporias... Vienna, Paris, and London are far away. Bosnia needs to be passed...

Keywords: Bosnia, aggression, Vienna, Paris, London, Mujahideen, Russians, Montenegrins, Animals

"All this, my dear, will be covered with snow, rosemary, and sedge."

---

1 Aporija – confusion, helplessness, ambiguity, logical difficulty, suspicious or disputable matter.

FOREWORD

How did this book come about?

Spontaneous. I found a geographical map of Southeast Europe, withdrawn five-pointed stars, published at a scientific conference in Zadar. Below it, I have written several historiographical facts, as recorded on Wikipedia. I posted it on Facebook. The debate began and flared up. I was careful. He asked if it made sense to put up such a map. The professor of history and humanities encouraged me. Set it up, feel free. Let people write what they think about everything. We all go through it and survive. Until Facebook burns us down.

I wrote down my experiences, views, and opinions, without a final judgment. I leave that judgment to the reader.

And the book.

I would like the cooperation of ethics and nobility in the human race to be achieved.

Will it? Why not so far? Is human knowledge increasing? Are we an open society? Have our spiritual and democratic horizons been expanded and purified? Have we freed ourselves and our spirit from the tutelage of authority and prejudice? Have we got rid of the self-born, the only absolute traditions based on tradition?

The author

CONTEMPORARY PHILOSOPHY

WE AND EUROPE - FROM AND TO WHEN?

Source: International Scientific Conference, Southeast Europe 1918 - 1995", Zadar 1995.

1. The First Balkan War

1912. and 1913. Kingdoms: Serbia, Bulgaria, Greece, Montenegro v. Turkey, Ottoman Empire, nine months. In the end, the independent state of Albania was created.

2. The Second Balkan War

1913. The Kingdom of Bulgaria against the Kingdom of Serbia, Greece, Montenegro, and the Ottoman Empire, forty-two days, in the middle of 1913. Serbia became the dominant power in the Balkans.

3. World War I

1914 to 1918 Austro-Hungarian monarchy (Central Powers) against Serbia and Montenegro (Triple Entente) Austro-Hungary disintegrated. The Kingdom of Serbs, Croats, and Slovenes was created. The Kingdom of Montenegro has disappeared.

1929 The Kingdom of Yugoslavia is created.

4. Georgi Dimitrov

In 1933, at the trial in Leipzig, he publicly defended himself against the accusation that he set fire to the Reichstag. (Out of Europe.) Now, publicly, they are judging Shishmakov, here.

5. World War II

1941 to 1945 Germany, Italy with its allies against Yugoslavia. (Out of Europe.)

1943, November 29, AVNOJ.

On May 9, Fascism was defeated. (Out of Europe.)

On May 15, Yugoslavwas is liberated.

6. The Third Balkan War continues…

27.6. to 7/6/1991 The war in Slovenia.

1991 to 1995 Homeland War in Croatia. (Franjo Tuđman van Europe.)

On 9/8/1991 Macedonia declared independence.

1992 to 1995. War in Bosnia and Herzegovina.

27.4.1992 A fragmented Yugoslavia was created.

07.02.1992 The Maastricht Treaty established European Union.

In 2006, Montenegro separated from Solania – FRY – what it was as the rest of Yugoslavia.

2008. Unilaterally seceded Kosovo.

Everything outside of Europe.

7.   CONVERSATION

She first found out about the Slovenes. She realized that they were different from Her. We called them Slovenes because they are different from us. They, for themselves, still say that they are Slavs.

They kept, in speech, in his language duality. We, in our speech, in our language have only the singular and the plural. We rarely say that we are Slavs. Europe doesn't care much about that.

From 1912 until now, Europe has had no idea who, what peoples live, and whether they live in the Balkans. In any case, she accepted, she attracted Slovenes, then Croats... Bulgarians, Greeks. These others, if there are any, the question is whether and when. Everything was and will be without Her knowledge and Her guilt. They bring Presheren and Njegosh closer in the same way they brought them together when I was a child. The nations parted and separated. They have not yet managed to unite. It doesn't matter until they return beyond the Carpathians, Polablje, and Pomorje, around the Baltics, it doesn't matter. (Out of Europe.) Tomorrow after tomorrow. (Out of Europe.)

Elijah of Thunder

NDBiH:

The answer to your poor and incomprehensible text is that you renamed the conflicts and confused the culprits and victims of the liberation and conquest wars to erase the facts. I read it quickly, I don't believe I made a mistake in assessing your intention, which you could have written clearly. 23 years since the genocide in Srebrenica. Bosniaks have experienced 10 genocides in their history.

The first genocide:

It happened to Muslims in the period from 1683 to 1699. This is the first, great tragedy for the Bosniak-Muslim people. It happens during and after the great Viennese war between the Turkish Empire and Austria. In that war, the Turks lost all their possessions and power in Hungary, Slavonia, Lika, Krbava, Dalmatia, and the Bay of Kotor. All Muslims from these areas, who failed to withdraw in time to Bosnia and other areas south of the Sava and Danube, were killed, expelled, assimilated, and converted to the Catholic faith. The organizer of that genocide was the Catholic Church. All monuments of Islamic civilization: mosques, bezistens, khans, libraries, caravanserais, tekkes, turrets, and madrasas were demolished and destroyed. During the previous 160 years of Muslim rule, not a single church or cathedral was destroyed in those areas. Christian Catholics enjoyed all human, religious, cultural, and property rights. Instead of gratitude and tolerance towards Muslims, Christians in those parts, in the name of their religion, seem to be the creators of the earth, not God. In all this, the most important thing is to say that Turkey and Austria were at war and that the victims were Bosniak Muslims.

The Second genocide:

It happens to Muslims in 1711, on the eve of Christmas Eve. That night, the so-called "investigation of poturica" was carried out. Thousands of Muslims were killed, and a small number fled to Nikšić and the village of Tuđemile near Bar. The organizer of that genocide, which took place in the area of Old Montenegro, was the Orthodox Church, not the Catholic Church. All the motives for that genocide were sung in "The Mountain Wreath."

The Third genocide:

It happened to Muslims in the period from 1804 to 1820, in Serbia, as a consequence of the First and Second Serbian Uprising. The key role in this genocide against Muslims was played by the Orthodox Church, Serbian historians, politicians, and poets like Njegosh. In 1804, Karadjordj's insurgents attacked the Bosniak – the Muslim population of Sjenica and killed about 5,000 Muslims – massacring children, the elderly, and women.

Fourth genocide:

It happened to Muslims in the period from 1830 to 1867, as a consequence of the Hatisherif of 1830, by which Serbia gained the status of vassal autonomy within the Ottoman Empire. Therefore, the possibility of emigrating and expelling Bosniak Muslims from Uzice, Cacak, Sabac, Sokol, and Belgrade. Porta settled all these Bosniak Muslims in Bosnia – Bosanski Samac and Orasje.

The Fifth genocide:

Over Muslim Albanians and Bosniaks, it happened in the period from 1876 to 1878, in Serbia and Montenegro. By the decisions of the Berlin Congress, Serbia and Montenegro gained full independence and significantly expanded their territories. Thus, Serbia expanded territorially in the districts of Niš, Pirot, Toplica, and Vranje, and Montenegro in Herzegovina (Nikšić, Grahovo, Bileća, and Trebinje). Toplica and Vranje regions were inhabited by a large percentage of Albanian Muslims. Today, they are not in those areas at all. In just 16 years, in the period from 1862 to 1878, several hundred mosques, many clock towers, libraries, inns, and bezistans in Belgrade, Sabac, Uzice, Sokol, Nis, Pirot, Prokuplje, Kursumlija, and Vranje. Tens of thousands of Bosniak and Albanian Muslims were expelled and killed. In 1876, the town of Nikšić was inhabited by 98% Bosniak Muslims, but in 1879 this town was left without Bosniaks, because the Muslims of Nikšić moved to the Great Muhajiluk towards Turkey, Sandžak, Albania, Kosovo, and Bosnia. All this was under the pressure of the new Montenegrin government, which showed Bosniaks - Muslims the way to Turkey. Thus, the Muslims of Nikšić, with great pain, left their van and all headed to the deserted parts of Anatolia, never to return because they did not want to be judged by Kaurin.

The Sixth genocide:

Over the Muslims, the period from 1878 to 1910, as a consequence of the Austro-Hungarian occupation of Bosnia and Herzegovina. During this period, a large wave of Bosniak Muslims began in Sandzak, Turkey, Kosovo, and Macedonia, where, at that time, there was still Turkish rule.

Seventh genocide:

It happened to the Muslims of Sandzak and Montenegro, as an attempt to forcibly baptize Muslims in Plav and Gusinje. The balance of the victims, those who did not want to be baptized, is such that were taken in bukagi to the place of Previja near Andrijevica, where 850 of them were shot. In those days, in Gusinje, 12,500 Bosniaks and Albanians were baptized. The consequences were the First and Second Balkan Wars (1912- 1913).

The Eighth genocide:

Above the Muslims, it lasted from 1918 to 1941, in the Kingdom of Serbs, Croats, and Slovenes. In that Kingdom and the Kingdom of Yugoslavia, the lives of Bosniak and Albanian Muslims were of no value. They were exposed to a genocide in Sandzak, Herzegovina, Montenegro, and Kosovo. For example, in the village of Šahovići, Bijelo Polje municipality, Sandžak, on November 7, 1924, on Eid al-Adha itself, 2,500 Bosniak Muslims were killed by Montenegrins for no apparent reason. According to the memories of the surviving Bosniaks, they heard

11

a Montenegrin, when he saw an old Muslim slaughtering a sacrificial animal, say to another next to him: „Look at that Turk slaughtering a lock. The lock will be ours." He hung out the innocent old man and skinned him alive, took out his heart, and threw it to the dog to eat. The dog smelled and did not want to eat the heart. Then the butcher said: "Not even a dog wants a Turkish heart!" Everything is clear that there is nothing more to talk about. Animals do not do what they did. Thousands of Bosniaks in Herzegovina and Montenegro, as well as Albanians in Kosovo, were killed as planned. Nobody was responsible for that. All this was done with the aim of ethnic cleansing, changing ethnic maps, and moving Muslims to Turkey. In 1925, 50,000 Bosniaks emigrated from several Sandzak cities to Turkey.

The Ninth genocide:

It happened to Muslims in the period from 1941 to 1945. World War II took 103,000 Muslim lives. Most Muslims were killed by a Chetnik, a neighbor's knife, which reached them on the doorstep, in the courtyard, and in the field. Muslims did not oppose their butchers and villains with the weapon in the first nine genocides.

The Tenth genocide:

He is the greatest and most cruel to Muslims in Bosnia and Herzegovina. It started in April 1992 and lasted until 1995. This war was being prepared for a long time, and it was taking place in front of the whole world. Serbia, Montenegro, and Croatia are participating against a small Bosniak Muslim people in Europe to destroy it. For the first time in history, the Bosniak Muslim people, in the heart of the Balkans, are organizing their army, police, and state to oppose the most modern armies of Europe and the world, to defend and survive in the heart of Europe. This war, in the period from 1992 to 1995, swallowed 250,000 Muslims. The Albanian-Muslim people experienced the same fate from the Chetnik army, during 1998/99. years.

ELIJAH OF THUNDER:

Dear and highly respected NDBiH, I thank you for your very rich answer. The purpose of my poor and incomprehensible text is not to obliterate the facts. I don't know what conflicts I renamed. I don't know which culprits and victims I confused. I did not know about the first genocide (1683 to 1699) until I read what You wrote. Am I concluding correctly if I say that Turkey and Austria are to blame for this genocide?

Were they outside Europe then?

For the second genocide (1711), I do not deny your claim that this genocide was organized by the Orthodox Church, not the Catholic Church. Njegosh could not have arranged it because he lived, approximately, 100 years after 1711. If he hadn't sung it, it might not even be known that it happened. He didn't hide it. He belonged to the Orthodox Church. Is there an Orthodox Church in Europe? Out of Europe?

I do not deny the third genocide (1804 to 1820). I accept that the facts are as you described them.

I did not know about the fourth genocide (1830 to 1867) until I read how you described it. Am I concluding correctly if I say that the culprit is the Ottoman Empire, which was prescribed by Hatisherif in 1830, thus enabling this genocide to happen? Was it outside Europe?

I accept the fifth genocide (1876 to 1878) as you described it. Was he outside Europe too? Who made it possible?

I accept the sixth genocide (1878 to 1910) as you described it. You say that, for him, Austria-Hungary is to blame. Is Austria- Hungary outside Europe?

I did not know about the seventh genocide (1912 to 1913, I and II Balkan Wars), which you described. Was he out of Europe too? Has Europe done something preventive to prevent it from happening?

I accept the eighth genocide (1918 to 1941) as you described it. Was he outside Europe too?

I accept the ninth genocide (1941 to 1945) as you described it. Out of Europe?

I accept the tenth genocide (April 1992 to 1995) as you described it. Out of Europe?

The title of my poor and incomprehensible text is: "WE and EUROPE from and until when?" I watch. In it, short sentences, I only mentioned the names of some events from 1912 to the present day. I listed the names as they are written on Wikipedia. I arranged them in chronological order: I and II Balkan War, World War I, Georgi Dimitrov, World War II, III Balkan War, and I added, later the Berlin Congress, which was in the 19th century. Based on my modest knowledge, these are the facts that are so named in historiography.

I ask: Which conflict did I rename? Which culprits and victims did I confuse? Which liberation and conquest wars did I confuse? Why did you come out of the period from 1912 to the present day, which I have indicated, knowing that the period of consideration can be much, much wider?

In my poor, incomprehensible text, I do not mention any of what you wrote and I do not deny what you wrote. Can you answer the questions I asked?

Reserve questions: Is the modern Independent State of Bosnia and Herzegovina in Europe, ie in the European Union? If not, why not? When will? Where is he now? Are they, the culprits for genocides you are writing about, in Europe or outside Europe? Is it us, us, or are we outside Europe? If you can, answer these reserved questions for me.

With respect.

NDBiH

I did not write my text, I copied it. I don't know how to shorten a lot of facts, which we all know and all interpret differently. I wouldn't spread it. I'm not into digging into ancient history. Honestly, I don't even care what my great-grandfather was, let alone someone else's. I know that Yugoslavia was like a mother to us. We were all happy in it and loved each other, trusted each other, and we're like brothers, one people. In short, we were much better than today's EU, which we would all like to enter so that the current madness would stop. It is an indisputable fact that Milosevic and Serbia disintegrated Yugoslavia. He walked around Kosovo and threatened anyone who attacked the (non-attacked) Serb people, and at the same time, non-Serbs on military service were found killed in barracks throughout the Yugoslav People's Army. When it was not accepted for all Republics to be under the cap of Serbia, there was a split, leaving the session. Slovenia left YU, which ceased to exist with its exit. Then Croatia came out, and after the military attack on Slovenia, Serbia (it was no longer the JNA) attacked Croatia. The world recognized both of these Republics, and a little later, upon request, BiH. Then all Serbian and Montenegrin garbage fell on BiH. These were Chetnik's hordes of evil. They took off their five-legged friends, put on cockades, tore themselves apart, messy, dirty. They let go of their beards and hair. They attacked Dubrovnik and Ravno. They bombed Mostar. They strengthened by appropriating JNA weapons, which disappeared after killing young men in the barracks. Montenegrins raided Herzegovina. Arkanovci and Seseljevci surrounded the hills and shot at people and animals. People without food, water, electricity, and medicine. Typical terrorism over the BiH capital. And, the people rose to the defense, without weapons ... and so on. Everything is known, what evils happened, and culminated in genocide ... Then came the stupid Dayton Accords. As soon as it was signed by "those who were not aggressors" (Milosevic and Tudjman), the war ended. How, when they were not involved? And let's not forget. They, the three signatories, and most of all Alija are to blame for the current situation in BiH, because nationalists, Chetniks, and Ustashas are still hoping for success, hunting in the dark. Their separatist dreams will never come true. Most of us, both attackers and defenders, will die sooner. Now, who is the positive, and who is the negative? Those who die in their own country and on their doorstep, or those who come from another country to rob and kill in another country. It should be said that the Montenegrins escaped hypocritically without punishment for their criminals. Yes, yes, there were those from outside who joined the war. It was the Russians the most. There were also mujahideen. God knows what happened to us, who intertwined his fingers, for some of his various private interests. Et cetera. But there is only one real, true culprit for both the disintegration of Yugoslavia and the war - Serbia led by Milosevic and the project of a Greater Serbia and domestic traitors. I apologize if I have offended you personally and unintentionally in some way.

With respect.

ELIJAH OF THUNDER:

Dear NDBiH, I read what you copied and what you wrote.

You don't answer any of my specific questions. Neither unreserved nor spare. Will you? Can you? Do you know? Say it. You started in 1683 and ended with those, which are not worth mentioning, from the last decade of the 20th century. It's too long, too wide a period to be able to say, determine what is the cause and what is the consequence. So: answer my questions f irst. All. After that, we can, if we want, and we could also, about this last one, which you wrote.

With respect.

NDBiH:

I told you everything. Compare. What happened, and you didn't name it, I did. What you didn't write, I did. I didn't leave anything out as far as the time or our life is concerned.

For example, for you it was the war in BiH, for us it was the aggression of Serbia on BiH. He was in Croatia, I can't remember, "as a Homeland War" and they defended against Serbian aggression. Kosovo did not secede unilaterally, but by fighting freed itself from the aggression of the SAF on the Autonomous Province and liberated the people of Kosovo from Serbian terror. You did not write that BiH is recognized as the Sovereign State of all peoples in it, and so on. I just don't understand what this "outside of Europe" and the like means.

With respect.

ELIJAH OF THUNDER:

Dear NDBiH, I do not dispute any of your terms or names. I told you that I copied the terms from Wikipedia. These are not the terms I coined. Terminology and names should be harmonized with it (Wikipedia). I repeat: I do not dispute or argue with the terms you have used here. So, if anyone is to blame for the terms, it's Wikipedia. The point of my text was not to talk about what you wrote, but it's nice to talk about it. You are wrong when you say that it is something to me that you think it is. Do you want to continue the conversation? To return to the topic of my text? What you wrote is off-topic.

NDBIH:

Not everything that is found on Wikipedia and the Internet is true or true. In this case, we don't need it. We know for ourselves what happened to us in the time in which we live. About the past, we can read, and believe it or not.

ELIJAH OF THUNDER:

Dear NDBiH, two people liked my text. One of them is a professor of history in Bugojno. He graduated from the Faculty of Philosophy in Sarajevo. You skipped that fact.

Our entire conversation is off-topic. I'm not saying that everything is true and true that can be found on Wikipedia and the Internet. That could be true of what we are talking about.

I do not contradict, dispute, or replicate any of the facts you have stated or the notion you have named. I think that the consequence of everything that happened and happened is the situation we have now. Is that so? Is this condition good?

I read, again, your last words. I compare and ask:

1. If there was the aggression of Serbia on BiH, the Homeland War in Croatia, everything was defended against Serbian aggression (which I do not dispute), does that mean that it was not a war and that there were no wars? Was it in Europe? Out of Europe?

2. If Kosovo did not secede unilaterally but freed itself from the aggression of the SAF (What is the SAF?) Against the Autonomous Province and liberated the people of Kosovo from Serbian terror (which I do not dispute, but I do not know who terrorized whom there), does that mean that it is not in Europe either? Out of Europe?

3. I did not write that BiH is recognized as a sovereign state of all peoples in it, but I did not deny it. What does this fact mean and what is the purpose? Is it in Europe? Out of Europe?

4. Did you correct all the wrong names? What is the purpose of these corrections? What is the purpose of the omitted, important facts-truths you are talking about?

5. What do Croats and Slovenes say about the topic we are discussing?

With respect.

NDBiH

I'm glad the professor of history liked your text. For all of us (Muslims, Catholics, Orthodox, Jews, Roma...) the most important thing is that, if you are already describing all the wars, describe the war in BiH as the aggression of Serbia with Montenegro, and that, this war, is a terrible genocide of Muslims. That's why the professor liked the text, which you wrote, but you hid important facts, which should not be skipped. It is important that the whole world knows and that it is written, that they come and pay their respects at so many cemeteries of the monstrously killed. I do not want the daily rhetoric of the aggressors in BiH to be heard. I'm not happy to argue about that. That is over and recorded.

ELIJAH OF THUNDER:

Dear NDBiH, I am not a historian. Are you? The meaning of my text was not to describe the war in BiH. I don't know, I don't think, I don't dare and I wouldn't be able to describe that war. That is why I do not engage in describing it, nor in describing other wars. I leave it to the people who are competent for it. If you are competent, I am glad that you write and describe. You can ask my opinion, as a non-expert, in this area. The best I know about the war in BiH is to ask.

For our conversation, I am writing to you:

17

FROM THE DURMITOR I AM CALLING

It doesn't matter where you come from,

how old you are,

do you know how to ski,

are you alone or in company,

I have room for everyone

and you are always welcome.

Here is not droped by,

than comes,

stays enjoys, rejoices,

and always returns.

Eagle

Discover Montenegro - National Park Durmitor[1]

---

1   Source: https://www.discover-montenegro.com/durmitor/

In the next chapter, you will find out what Elijah of Thunder did and what happened to him at the time when Montenegrins, together with the Mujahideen, Russians, and all the other animals, were marching around Bosnia, how he managed to escape, sneakily and unpunished, hidden and unnoticed, in a group with the rest, remaining Catholics, Orthodox, Muslims, and Roma, who were not aggressors in the NDBiH. You will learn that he was saved personally by Richard Holbrooke, although he only later heard of the term "holbrooking in Bosnia", and it took him a long time to think, translate and interpret to understand the term meant.

MICROCOSM
— Flight over the cuckoo's nest —

July is 1980. Head of the Medical Devices Service. The hospital, surprisingly, is full of extraordinary, diverse, challenging electronic devices. Elijah cannot determine what is more interesting: coronary unit, intensive care, X-ray, biochemical laboratory, sodium-potassium pump, flame photometry, gas analysis, ...

He immersed himself in the work, very motivated. He chose, decided, to formally confirm his elan. He enrolled in postgraduate studies in biomedical and clinical engineering at the University of Belgrade. Topics for work and research more than much. More and more interesting than each other. Electrophysiological signals, electroencephalography, electromyography, biopotentials, gas analysis, sodium potassium pump, flame photometry...

The main medical engineering project, at that time in the Microcosm, was the X-ray Computed Tomography acquisition project. In order not to research something that is not the mainstream in his postgraduate studies, and therefore to play the role of an outlier in the environment in which he came to work, which he did not want, he focused on X-ray computed tomography. Logically and spontaneously, he was joined by other methods of medical imaging, magnetic resonance imaging, gamma cameras, PET and SPECT scanners, ultrasound scanners...

He was appointed a member of the commission for the selection of the best supplier of X-ray computed tomography. He studied the offers of the world's largest manufacturers very studiously, in the domain that belonged to him. All offers were good. The Commission would not have been wrong to have chosen any of the offers. After studious analysis and comparisons, Elijah liked the offer of the General Electric tomograph fr Milwaukee, USA, whose representative and importer was "Jugolek" from Belgrade. He thinks that his analysis and presentation of offers contributed to the choice of the computer tomograph of that manufacturer.

One, one might say, funny detail happened. This computed tomography was so good, so perfect, it passed so many quality control tests, extremely high protection systems against ionizing radiation, both the device itself and the room in which it was installed, that it is difficult to enumerate, let alone describe briefly. Like spaceship.

For such a device, the republican microcosm law stipulated that it could not be put into operation without a professor from the physics laboratory of the „Veljko Vlahović" University in Titograd measuring the level of ionizing ra diation in the space where it was installed. The professor did it. He measured the level of ionizing radiation with his primitive instrument. Thus, the chosen computer tomograph passed that inspection and received a work permit.

There are other interesting details about that tomograph. The manufacturer, General Electric, provided one month of training for two engineers at its Milwaukee plant. All at General Electric's expense. Elijah thought and believed that such training belongs to him. He was not only entitled to that training, but he was entitled to and fulfilled much more than basic conditions required by General Electric. That tomograph was in the description of his jobs and work tasks. In his jurisdiction. By priority and essence. But, very poetically, a miracle happened. He didn't receive training and didn't go to that training. Two other engineers left.

What kind of miracle happened? It is necessary, indeed, that a divine spark shines, a ray of light in the darkness illuminates this miracle. This can only be explained by the light from the "Light of the Microcosm". First, how was it decided that these two go to that training, and secondly, what did these two engineers do later and how much was the reward of free training binding them? Or is it not for free? Or did they do something for it? This is a problem from the domain of "Light of the Microcosm" and the Microcosm, in which Elijah also found himself. He does not know. He can't understand. He doesn't understand how and in what way the two of them agreed with Abbot Stefan, who decided on it. Elijah remembers that the two of them got into fighting while training in Milwaukee. He heard that it was being discussed in the office of Abbot Stefan. He remembers that one of the two of them, the younger one, left the Hospital very quickly and went to Belgrade to work there. The older one died a little later, but soon after that. Thus, General Electric's computer tomograph remained "professionally unserviced."

Elijah did not regret that he did not go to Milwaukee, to the General Electric factory, at the expense of General Electric, but he was surprised and confused. The only requirement that General Electric set for the engineers it trained was that they have a basic knowledge of electrical engineering. Elijah had much more than that basic knowledge. According to the systematization of work and according to the principles of unalienated social work, which ruled at that time, it belonged to him. Because of all that and what happened, he can only wonder and be confused. Abbot Stefan is not anyone! He is from the head of the whole nation.

Even later, at some of the gatherings of "unalienated social work" Abbot Stefan used to criticize Elijah personally, saying that he did not „become famous as an engineer".

Abbot Stefan did not have the slightest understanding, not even compassion for Elijah. In addition, he had to take care of cardiology and the health of heart patients in the Microcosm, take care of the copyright protection of the architects of the New Hospital building and many other things. Thus, in all this, Elijah can understand the reasons why it is not easy to achieve the status of Abbot Stefan. Abbot Stefan is not getting easy! It is from the head of the whole nation, but it is notrelevant.

As if nothing had happened, Elijah continued to try to find himself in the Microcosm where he was. He regulary came to work and worked. He also managed to find time for post-graduate studies, which he enrolled voluntarily. In their postgraduate studies in the field of cell biology, human physiology, and, elements of biophysics... he was evaluated with the highest marks, tens. Only a professor from his home faculty gave him a grade of nine. The professor questioned him in the office, on a "one on one" basis. About twenty questions. Elijah did not answer one of these questions perfectly, and that was enough for the professor to rate him only a nine. The question and answer were related to protection against electric shock in underwater massage tubs in physical therapy. Elijah had neither the courage nor the time to cancel that nine. He was strict with himself, no less strict than the professors from his home faculty, and if they were strict, they were.

What happened next? There was a war. Refugees came. From Bosnia... The director became the famous Primarius Anemic, later long-time president of the Medical Chamber. He applied the generally accepted principle of the Microcosm: "When the people are not angry, the house is not cramped." According to this principle, which was implemented by the induced authorities of the Microcosm, as well as according to international law, which is incorporated into the State, refugees are not a burden. They are people who bring the missing knowledge, especially from informatics, medicine... They will enrich the environment they came to. The Anemic Director, in addition to other examples where he applied the same principle "when the people are not angry, the house is not cramped," he accepted into the service, to which Elijah also belonged, a refugee, they said, from Bosnia, from Sarajevo.

The refugee also did what was not in his job description, for which he received a salary. He was spying. This skill, it seems, could not be expressed where he came from, but that is why it was in the Microcosm, into which he escaped.

In the period from December 1 to 31, 1992, Elijah was "absent" from work. The virtuous employer Anemic Director and Refugee knew that Elijah was "absent" from work and they wrote him down "In absent", but Elijah did not know that he was "absent" and that they were writing him "in absent" from work. A virtuous employer, Anemic Director, with full-time work and a head full of care for the sick, in addition to his commitment to the vocation, sought, Elijah, everywhere, where he could not find it. Only he didn't look for him where he could find him. Not healthy enough, but physically not far from him, a virtuous employer the Anemic Director. Everything according to law... the virtuous employer Anemic Director learned and negotiated directly from Hippocrates. Examples of humanity and heroism are intended for animals from Bosnia. Everything was by the Code of Medical Ethics and Deontology, which the Anemic Director will issue 16 years later. Such was the time. Ethics have changed. He could not betray ethics before he changed. Until then, it is based on the principle "you don't die from it". He wisely said to Elijah, in his office as the director of the KBC: "Science is at the faculties," "Are you doing this with us?" Pure philosophy, popularly speaking.[2]

When, by chance, he learned that he was being absent, Elijah, in panic, rushed to a psychiatrist, where he occasionally came to therapy and to the Health Center, to get sick leave, which was recommended by a psychiatrist, but there was no salvation or help.

What people are not angry? Which house is not cramped? Whose house? Who fought? Where? Who was left without a job, personal

---

2   To this pictorial description of the Anemic Director, Elijah adds a sense of disgust, contempt, and indifference, which are uselessly mixed when he meets or thinks of the Anemic Director on the street, a virtuous civil servant of the Microcosm.

income, salary, or social protection? On the street with three minor children of school-age... The people will gild it all. (Laza Lazarevic)

During the period when Elijah was "absent" from work, Elijah, as the main researcher, submitted an application for a scientific research project in the field of biomedical engineering to the Medical Institute of the University of Microcosm, the only scientific research institution, which is, at that time, existed in the Microcosm, for the field of medicine. The leader of that project was Magnetic Resonance Imager, who was working at the Military Medical Academy in Belgrade at the time, and one of the participants in the project was Academic IEEE, then a professor at the Faculty of Electrical Engineering in Podgorica. The president of the Scientific Council of that institute was Diabetes, a scientific advisor, and the director, the above- mentioned Abbot Stefan, also a scientific advisor. One of the members of the Scientific Council, among others, was, at that time, the Depressed Optimist, a scientific advisor. The Scientific Council concluded, in the form of a sentence, supporting Elijah's initiative for the project and proposed to the Medical Institute to take measures of program activities in the discipline from which the project originates. Evidence of this exists in the archives of that Medical Institute if that archive still exists. Cimbaljevic Primarius Dr. Milos said: we don't need that. Diabetes said: Everything you want, we buy as a finished product. (In other words, they were operated out of personal participation in technological development, though they weren't. Diabetes significantly contributed to the purchase of that apparatus for hormone analysis.)

The room from which Elijah was "absent" is located in the basement of the Microcosm Clinical Hospital Center, across from the hospital kitchen. The premises of the Medical Institute were in the building of the current Institute of Public Health. Between that part of the building and the KBC building, from which Elijah "was absent," without knowing that he was "absent" is a road - a slightly wider asphalt strip, which leads from the main entrance to the hospital yard on the left, toward the basement, where it that time there was a department for polyclinic x-ray diagnostic, computed tomography, on the right and hematology, on the left. Two adjacent buildings, about thirty meters apart, as the crow flies, from each other. The office of the Anemic Director Primarius was in the same place where the KBC director's office is now, on the first floor, rougly and almost directly above the room from which Elijah was "absent." All this took place with the knowledge and under the direct control of Hippocrates.

In addition, this is a concrete example of how Montenegrins, together with the Mujahideen and the Russians, invaded Bosnia and attacked and carried out aggression against the NDBiH, while poor and above all professional refugees, "not by their own choice," fled from war-torn areas and brought missing knowledge to the Microcosm. Elijah does not rule out the possibility, He even believes, that they brought the same knowledge to other areas where they, poor people, were fleeing from aggressors and others who were at war.

That's not all. Mara Drecun, also found accommodation in that house, at the same time as the Unfortunate Refugee Spy. One and a half, two floors above Elijah's head, which might not even existed. On the same floor as the Anemic Director. Very close to him.

Tell us, grandma, are you a witch!!!??

Everything you read is not relevant. Mara is not NDBiH. Mara is the Dependent State of BiH. Maybe it has nothing to do with BiH? Who knows!? Maybe the Vlachs will never figure it out. Why didn't Ms. NDBiH create the conditions for Mara to treat her, NDBiH, until the end of Mara's career? Instead, Ms. NDBiH created Mara, so she sent Mara to heal the Microcosm. Did Mara study physiology from the Bosnian dictionary of Muhamed Hevai Uskufi from 1631?

About Mara, "Staff of Special Interest," can be read in detail[3]. There, learned people, who did not follow the rules of the province in which they live, said that Mara was not a staff of "first-class professional and scientific importance for the Institution." Arrogant "Trebinjci" is a generally accepted name for angry refugees from BiH. What? Are you saying that Mara and the Escaped Spy are not arrogant? Is she not employed to be the head (director) of the KBC Development Institute? Then. That year. That, all that, is irrelevant? Did she only and mostly write and publish textbooks Has she written or published anything of value in biomedical engineering?

Let's leave her, for a moment, alone. Let's look, many years later, at the Main Board for Medical Research in the Microcosm. Look at the miracles! Magnetic Resonant Imager, Diabetes, KKK2, Anemic Director, here they are, along with Mara, on that board. Nothing has changed. Medicine has not been researched.

---

3 Darko Suković, „Refugees - Danger or Potential", AIM, Montenegro, Mon, 07 Mar 1994 22:36:01 GMT.

CONCLUSION

The most important Drecuni are from Ljubotinje. Is Mara their daughter or daughter-in-law?

The most important relatives and descendants of the Anemic Director are from Martinić. Here they are, the Anemic Director, to be proud of him! That he celebrates, instead of them, the battle of Martinići. It is his and only his battle and victory. He won it with a heroic, constant struggle in the field of Hematology. Although don't sin your soul, red blood cells grow in Martinići as well. It was such a time. The most important ancestors of the Refugee Spy are here, from Dahna, from Zeta. Maybe from another, a nearby village. Didn't they look for each other?[4]

WHO CAN COME HOME?

Long live the local priests! They, conscientiously, turn over and raise awareness of the bones of the killed Chetniks in the Microcosm.

DO YOU KNOW WHAT THE RELATIONSHIP BETWEEN WHAT YOU READ AND THE TOPICS IS?

The relationship is a failure. No one, no one, absolutely no one, has, not even in mind, biomedical engineering. He said, Milos, a long time ago: We don't need that. They said a long time ago: We buy all this as a finished product.

Should important people, who, in the chain of deciding on the issues of life and death of an individual, should be reminded that they have not died yet?

Remaining on the street, Elijah was assisted by Sadako Ogata and the United Nations High Commissioner for Refugees. He was forced to work for them for the benefit of refugees. According to the work contract. This was an additional contribution to the care of refugees. The previous contribution was, as you can see, being out of a job, for the benefit of a refugee. Elijah did all that without war, without struggle. He was not in the war. He did not run away, avoid, or save his life,

---

4 No no no! Error!!! A big!!! They're not from Dahna! These are from Savnik! Is it, Savnik, a wolf fucker? And he did not escape from Sarajevo, but from Zagreb, but that is not entirely certain. Aww!!! It is not true that he is from Savnik, but a settlement near Plužine, in 1991, 59 inhabitants, and in 2003, 22 inhabitants. During the treatment of the post-traumatic syndrome caused by this event, a clinical psychologist, a specialist in clinical psychology, listened in silence. In the end, she said, "I would fight with them."

from the war. He survived in the town of Podgorica, not moving, not alienated from his homeland. Montenegrins are attacking Bosnia, and Bosnia needs to be passed. Switzerland is far away... Elijah remembers, reminds, repeats over and over again, because, someone told him that these were the events that marked his life, he went to psychotherapy with a specialist in clinical psychology. He told her what the Refugee had done to him together with the Anemic Director, who was also her director. The psychologist told him that she would treat herself by fighting with them.

Before this "absence" from work, Elijah heard, yes, yes, you read that right, Elijah heard with his ears, from the office of the Anemic Director, that he could be appointed the leader of the team, which should bring washing machines, for laundry at the Hospital, as spoils of war from a hotel in Kupari. He was shocked by the idea and the opportunity to be given such an honor, to be determined for such a job. This idea has not been disclosed or realized, but, in the reconstruction and retrospective of the event, it is not out of place to express it.

When could it be that the washing machines from the hotel in Kupari were stolen? The machines were brought and leaned against the wall of KBC Mikrokosm.

The employer of the Anemic Director was the Hepatobiliary Surgeon, who applied the acquired knowledge of hepatobiliary surgery in the politics of the Microcosm, and his employer was a Tall Man Who Sees Highly Through the Microcosm.

At the Department of Forensic Medicine and Pathology lay the dead soldiers in torn, mud-stained JNA uniforms, brought from the battlefield in Čepikuće, where they had been ambushed. One of those soldiers was Ranko Bojic.

The wounded from the battlefield of aggressive or non- aggressive BiH (Is Bosnia where it used to be?) Were treated at the KBC Mikrokosmos.

WANTED LIST

Four persons are wanted, listed below.

These four faces are phantasmagorically, firmly, and inextricably bound by covalent bonds into one lump, which rolls through this world.

The mentioned persons were on the same jobs and tasks, on which they committed unexplored crimes.

All in all, it is indisputable that, in a joint criminal enterprise, they cleansed the country of the Unchristened.

DOWN

1. Unfortunate Spy Refugees from war-torn areas

2. Anemic Director Hippocrates

3. Hepatobiliary Surgeon

4. A Tall Man Who Sees High Through The Microcosm

PERSONS:

Abbot Stefan
Anemic Director
Chess Grandmaster
Magnetic Resonant Imager
Academician IEEE
Diabetes
Depressive Optimist
Laza Lazarevic
Sadako Ogata
Petar II Petrovic Njegos
Elijah

PLACE OF ACTION:

Medical Institute Titograd - Clinical Hospital Center of Montenegro

ACTIVITY TIME: 1980-1995

CONVERSATION

ElijaH's legal basis to pursue a profession or science was abolished. Because of that, he was left, as if forced, with the opportunity to deal with what is between the two, and that is philosophy. (Bertrand Russell)

The neurosurgeon says: I'm not crazy about philosophy until I look at X-rays, CT or NMR, and Mark Twain:

"It is easier to deceive a man than to convince him that he has been deceived."

SCENE

Hospital. Basement. The head nurse of Anesthesia runs. Distraught. Excited. Engineer, what about the gas blood gas analyzer???! Run! The patient is on the table! Elijah runs. First to the laboratory of the Main Hospital, then to the laboratory of the Children's Hospital. Apparatus for the analysis of partial pressures of blood gases, manufacured by AVL, Austria. Elijah can not figure out if they work or not. He runs back from Children's Hospital. A voice catchies up with him: the patient has died. The machine, in the Radoje Dakić's factory, cut off part of his forehead and brain. He was, for some, more than a distant cousin of Elijah, on his mother's side. In the basement of the Hospital, Elijah writes meaningless data on the parameters of the blood gas analysis device, in the technical card. He is sad. Exhausted. Fainted. Apparatus for gas analysis of blood and he. An undefined tear appears and does not appear in his eye. Is there an?

Today. Elijah meets prominent mayrs, specialists, and doctors of medical sciences on the street. They hang around private polyclinics, clinics, laboratories, and other private medical facilities, with licenses they got from Microcosm. Shops with their profession and their knowledge.

Light up the divine sparks, shine with light! Light them up above the Microcosm!

It remains to be determined whether, what was written, was copied from „Autobiography" of Branislav Nushich or from the sad fate of Rade Tomov from „The Light of the Microcosm" in the Cetinje monastery or in that monastery above Budva.

ELIJAH OF THUNDER AND
NDBiH CONTINUE

NDBiH:

Did you know:

1. That the first central heating was made in the Middle Ages, that thermal water was conducted from Fojnica to the royal fortress?

2. That Bosnia had public baths and hammams (today's saunas/baths) long before Paris and Europe?

3. That the first tram started in Sarajevo, only later in Vienna? Not to mention the rest of Europe ...

4. That Tvrtko Kotromanc was the first king of Bosnia, which, in his time, covered a large part of the Adriatic coast, all the way to Zadar, and that he built Herceg Novi?

5. That the first dictionary of the Bosnian language was published in 1631, about 180 years before the first Serbian dictionary, and 200 years before the first Croatian dictionary?

6. That Safet Sušić is the winner of the Order of the France Legion of Honor, as the best foreign player in France ever?

7. That Bosnia has Nobel laureates, Oscar winners ...?

8. That the first Internet news was sent to the world, for the first time, from Sarajevo at the 1984 Winter Olympics?

If you didn't know, don't forget to tell your children.

ELIJAH OF THUNDER:

What planet is this from?

NDBiH:

The planet is said and there are aliens among us.

ELIJAH OF THUNDER:

Shall we name those aliens among us? One by one... We don't have to list everything at once... gradually... as many as we recognize, and they are of interest to us...?

NDBiH:

We know a lot, but not all at once. But what do we have now from all that when three shepherds with their parties/corporations destroyed absolutely everything, so we are not talking about successes but only about nationalist squabbling, and hatred between the same multireligious people, who, after all, do not even show that much religiosity? Only mutual hatred, pointing out insignificant differences, etc. We all have a lot of our own, common, historical and cultural to boast about. It is sad what people in these areas are doing to themselves.

We all have a lot of ours, common, historical and cultural to brag about. It is sad what the people in this area are doing to themselves.

ELIJAH OF THUNDER:

Does anyone know which planets Asim Ferhatović, Ivica Osim, Josip Bukal, Vahidin Musemić are from ... Mirza Delibašić, Dražen Dalipagić ... Dušan Bajević, Franjo Vladić, Enver Marić ... Zaim Imamović, Beba Selimović, Emira Medunjanin ...are from?

NDBiH:

The only thing here is that in 1907 the Bosnian language was renamed Serbo-Croatian.

ELIJAH OF THUNDER:

Who renamed the Bosnian language in 1907? How? Why?

NDBiH:

The renaming was carried out by national-revolutionary movements from neighboring countries and the establishment of the first state within the Kingdom of Serbs, Croats, and Slovene when Bosniaks were deprived of the right to declare themselves as such but only as Serbs or Croats. And why? Well, that has been clear to everyone for a long time...

ELIJAH OF THUNDER:

What national-revolutionary movements, from neighboring countries, took place in 1907? In which country were Bosniaks in 1907? In which country, before the founding of the Kingdom of Serbs, Croats, and Slovenes in 1918, did Bosniaks have the right to declare themselves as Bosniaks? The Kingdom of Serbs, Croats, and Slovenes was founded in 1918, and here we are talking about 1907, the year when the Bosnian language was renamed. Who renamed the Bosniak language to Serbo Croatian? Who could have done that? It is unclear to me why Bosniaks were deprived of the right to declare themselves as Bosniaks, but only as Serbs and Croats, even though they had that right before. Please clarify ...

NDBiH:

The Bosniak language neither exists nor has ever existed. Bosniaks of the Islamic, Catholic, and Orthodox faith did exist, and the Bosnian language also existed. Do you know about the Bosnian Dictionary published in 1631? Or is it unknown to you?

ELIJAH OF THUNDER:

Not. I don't know what you are telling me, nor did I know. Please give me specific answers to the questions I asked, so we can harmonize all this and better understand what it is about. I do not know and do not understand the nuances between the terms: Bosnian and Bosniak.

NDBiH

Bosnian-Turkish dictionary: Muhamed Hevaji Uskufi

ELIJAH OF THUNDER:

Who published this dictionary? What are the Bosnian words in this dictionary? How different are they from the words in the modern Bosnian dictionary?

NDBiH:

It was published by Muhammed Hewai Uskufi, and we need more time for details.

ELIJAH OF THUNDER:

I am interested and I think it is very important. Many additional questions follow, such as: Who is Muhammad Hewai Uskufi? Could this dictionary have been used by neighboring nations to reach an agreement with the Turks and have they used it to reach an agreement with them?...

NDBiH:

Chronicle of Matica Srpska: First issue, 1985.

56	57
Here over ½ million in number, there are some Catholics and others east. orthodox. church. II, Slovene-Serbian koldno ?) 　To this koldnu belong: 　1. Bulgarians in the old kingdom of Bulgaria, and now in the so-called province of Sofia Vilaet, between the Danube, the Black Sea, the Balkans, and Serbia. From the Volga, they raised 679 and moved here, and there they visited the Slavic koldna which they suppressed, which in turn united with them, receiving the Slavic language and glory. Custom. There are about 500,000 Bulgarians; of which 450,000 are Orthodox Eastern Churches, and the rest are Catholics. 　2. The Serbs first lived in the Kingdom of Serbia (Present Province of Turkey) on both sides of the Morava between the Timok, Drina, Hema, Sava, and Danube rivers, especially at the end of the 17th century.	They crossed Hungary and settled there. They are abusive and Cancers are called from abroad; er iđva čast Serblâ živi oko rđke Rasci, koja e iđkad cđlu zemlju Cerbsku na Serbiju i Rasciju dđlila. There are 900,000 Serbs in Servovilaets; in Hungary, excluding Slavonia, 338,000; hence only 125,000: all are eastern. Orthodox church. 　3. Bosniaks live between the Drina, Vrbas, Sava, Dalmatia, and Hema, numbering 450,000: they profess either Islam or are Roman Catholics or Orthodox. 　4. Montenegrins are called Slavic inhabitants of the Montenegrin mountains in Turkish Albania, which stretches from the coast of Antivarsko to Bosnia. They were never conquered by the Turks: they are free and independent for today. They are managed by Bishop and Metropolitan Petr Petrović. There are also 53,000 people, all of whom are Orthodox. Church sons.

In this issue

The Chronicle of the Matica Srpska (Originally the Serbian Chronicle) for the year 1825 published a textbook about the tribes of the Slavic people. On p. 56 - 58. is the Slovene-Serbian tribe: Bulgarians, Serbs, (where everything is located; there are none in Montenegro), Bosniaks, Montenegrins, Slavonians, Dalmatians, and Montenegrins are Slavic inhabitants of the Montenegrin mountains...

ELIJAH OF THUNDER:

Based on this text of the Annals of the Matica Srpska, First
Issue, 1825, can it be concluded that Bulgarians, Serbs, Bosniaks,
Montenegrins... peoples of Slavic origin? How do they communicate
with each other? What are the differences between the languages they
speak?

NDBiH:

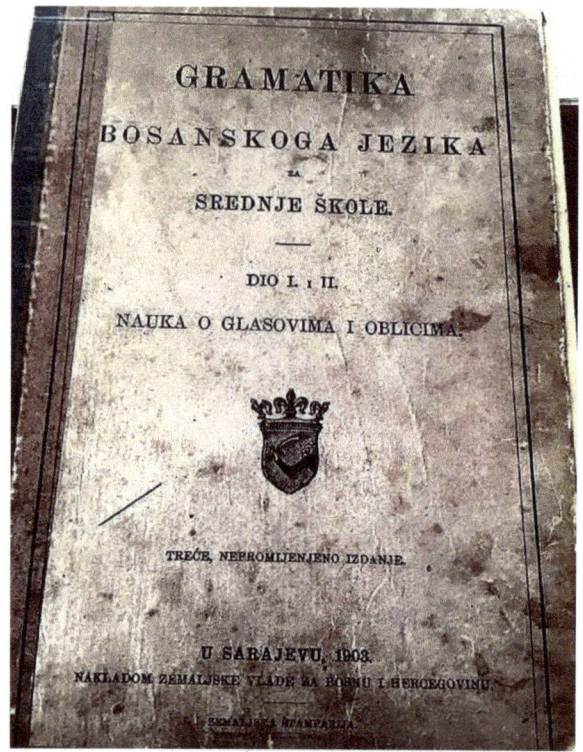

Bosnian language grammar

ELIJAH OF THUNDER:

I like this very much. I didn't know about this and this kind of
grammar.   I read and see that the publisher of this grammar is the
Provincial Government for Bosnia and Herzegovina, Sarajevo in 1903. I
am interested, and it is important: Which is the Provincial Government
in Bosnia and Herzegovina in 1903 and 1907? How and how much do
the voices, from this grammar, differ from the voices now in BiH and
from the voices in the surrounding, neighboring countries?

NDBIH:

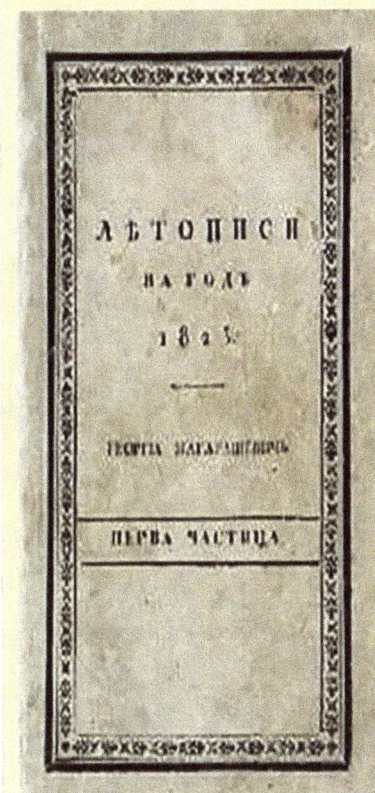

Bošnjaci žive izmeđ
Drine, Verbasa, Save,
Dalmacie i Hema
čislom 450.000,
ispovđdano
ili islam,
ili su rimokatolici,
ili pravoslavni.

"Letopis Matice srpske"
1825.

3. Бошняцы живе измеђ Дрине, Верба-
са, Саве, Далмацiе и Хема, числом 450000;
исповѣдаю или Ислам; или су Римокато-
лицы, или православни.

Cover of the Chronicle of Matica Srpska from 1825

ELIJAH OF THUNDER:

Did this chronicle dispute the existence of Bosniaks or did it confirm it? Does this chronicle dispute the right of Bosniaks to profess any religion, primarily Islamic, Roman Catholic, and Orthodox?

NDBiH:

Ilija Garashan's
DRAFT

The program of the foreign and national policy of Serbia at **the end of 1844**

<u>On the politics of Serbia and the review of Bosnia, Herzegovina, Montenegro, and Northern Albania.</u>

When we take a closer look at the geographical location of these countries, the war/ar spirit of their inhabitants, and take this opinion and their way of thinking closer, wewe will easily come to the conclusion that this is the part of the Turkish Empire on whichch Serbia can have the greatest influence. The constant determination and regulation of of this influence seem to us to be the main task of Serbian politics in Turkey for nowɔw (1844).

If **the Bosniaks** did not accept this, it would surely follow the dismembermentent of the Serbs into provincial small principalities under certain ruling families thatat would surrender to foreign and foreign influence, because they would compete withith each other and envy each other. These families would never allow themselves to be be led to sacrifice their interests to any other family, even if the progress of all theseɔse peoples depended on such sacrifice.

It follows from these principles that before this general **unification of Serbia,ia, especially in Bosnia, the transformation would begin, so that thehe transformation would seem to serve as a more prepared for the generalal unification of all Serbs and provinces at the same time,** which is the only way to to count on achieving that great goal and that interest which is equal to these Serbs -s - because here **I put Serbia forward only because it is the only one that canan prepare this thing and it is obliged to constantly nurture that the times that willill bring the implementation of this plan and what time to mature Serbia will to to do that.**

Therefore, whoever wishes good to these people, we must not recommend thehe hereditary princely dignity to **Bosniaks.** In such a case, the most important peopleple from the entire nation would be elected among them, and not for the rest of theirerir lives, but for a certain period of time, who would act as a council. With such an a provincial and separate government, the road to progress would remain open: **it it would be easy for Serbia to ally itself more closely with Bosnia in its time andnd be able to join forces** because then this alliance will remain possible and probable.le.

ELIJAH OF THUNDER:

What is the problem with this text? Does he dispute the existence of Bosniaks? Is it an evil desire, expressed in this text, for Serbia to be more closely connected and merged with Bosnia? Is it bad that it is not stated that each nation has its king Balakaha, who will promise his people that he will give them juhahaha, juhahaha, so each nation, in particular, will be able to sing, freely, according to their taste, juhahaha, juhahaha, because it is not promised by anyone, but by their King personally 13. Balakaha!

NDBiH:

DRAFT (Ilija Garashanin)

It will not be a difficult task for Serbia to have a greater influence **on Bosniaks in the Eastern religion**. More precaution and caution against this requires that **Catholic Bosniaks win**. At the head of these are the Franciscan friars.

In addition to the above-mentioned printing of books, wouldn't it be good and advisable for one of these Bosnian friars to be appointed to the Belgrade Lyceum as a professor of Latin and other sciences. This professor would have to serve as **a mediator between Serbia and the Catholics in Bosnia,** because with that they would take my first confidential step and with that they would give proof of tolerance. Couldn't this same friar establish a Catholic chapel here for the Catholics living here, which would avoid the erection of a chapel for the Catholics living here, which would avoid the erection of a chapel under the influence of the Austrians, which will sooner or later have to follow. This chapel could be placed under the auspices of the French consul living here. This would give an occasion and an opportunity to the French government to take a lively role in that matter, and thus Serbia would be free from the danger of a Catholic church, which would be under the influence of Austria in Belgrade.

Karadjordj was a rich military leader and very experienced: he could not foresee the great military importance that Montenegro has for Serbia and will always have a bitch whenever it comes **to Bosnia and Herzegovina separating from Turkey and joining Serbia.** . The march of this duke to Sjenica and Novi Pazar is still well remembered by all Serbs, and it is not necessary for us to support the following proposal with new arguments. In this way, Serbia will have the friendship of a country for a small price, which can deploy at least 10,000 mountain soldiers.

We must note here that the postponement of this support until the last moment will not have the desired success and consequence: since Russia will be able to justly invoke its perennial and constant support, and the Serbian new proposal will be able to blacken and make more suspicious; and the Montenegrins would then say: The Serbs did not help us when we were in need, which is proof that they are not our friends, but only want to use us for now.

ELIJAH OF THUNDER:

Where is "THE OPPOSITE DRAFT", who wrote it, and what does it say? What is better in that "OPPOSITE DRAFT" than that what is written on this "DRAFT"? How is it planned to bribe the existing nations in that "CONTRADICTORY DRAFT"? How did the "OPPOSITE DRAFT" manage to bribe the existing nations, because this "DRAFT" clearly failed to bribe them?

39

CONVERSATION

ELIJAH OF THUNDER:

What is the difference between Bosniaks, Muslims, and Bosnians?

NDBiH:

Bosniak is the name of people, which arose from the medieval Bosnians, through linguistic evolution. For example, in the Middle Ages, there were Servs, then Serbs, and a few hundred years ago they became Serbs. Muslim is a religious affiliation imposed on Bosniaks during the former Yugoslavia. At that time, people preferred to declare themselves as Muslims with a capital M, instead of Serbs, Croats, and the like that had been imposed until then.

Today, Bosnians are the name for a nation, which consists of several "peoples" and religions!

ELIJAH OF THUNDER:

How accurate is the claim that Bosniaks, during their long history, had periods of Romanization and Slovenization without having a period of Islamization?

NDBiH:

The Turks brought democracy, not destroying other religions, as the Chetniks and Ustashas wanted the disappearance of Muslims in Bosnia and Herzegovina with genocide and crime.

ELIJAH OF THUNDER:

Here is what can be found on the Internet about what you said: Bosniaks were created by Islamization from the 15th century onwards, from the Bosnian people of Bogumil religion, as well as the population of the surrounding countries. The ideology and self-definition of

41

Bosniaks lag behind Serbs and Croats due to national unconsciousness. Bosniaks stopped any activity that would express their ethnicity. Very little literature in the vernacular - they switched to Oriental writing - Turkish (Turkish, Arabic, Persian - Iranian), Croats and Serbs NO!

ANTAEUS COMPLEX[5] AND GLOBALIZATION

I – ANTAEUS

Antaeus was a man, invincible in battle, as long as he stood firm on the earth, his mother. Heracles defeated him by lifting him from the ground, lifting him, and drowning him. Antaeus loved his people, nature, the land that fed him, and where he lived. Your own country provides security and self-confidence. Can these essential feelings be replaced by success in another world?

II – GLOBALIZATION

The most general and at the same time, the most complete definition of globalization is the gradual abolition of restrictions on the flow of goods, services, people, and ideas between different countries and parts of the world.

The first thing that can be noticed in that definition is that it refers to different countries and parts of the world. The next noticeable fact is that these restrictions are so great that they cannot be lifted immediately and all at once, but gradually. Furthermore, it cannot be seen, in this definition, whether all people on the Planet are equal, regardless of race, gender, or religious affiliation ... What can that mean? That the individual, the person, and his needs are invisible and irrelevant?

Let's start in reverse order, from the end to the idea.

---

5   The anthean complex is used, in psychology, to denote a man whose web of subconscious reactions, feelings, instincts, etc., remained created in the place of birth, or homeland, in which he felt powerful, as a child, similar to Anthea, a hero of Greek mythology. This leads to milder mental disorders, burdens, and unexpected, abnormal reactions.

Who creates the idea? Man. What can he do with that idea? At the moment, the situation is such that he cannot do anything with that idea.

After that free nothing, one can, freely, ask if he is a man? Where should he go? How? Can he do anyone a favor? What kind of service could that be? Does he own any kind of goods? Whose need could he satisfy with these goods? Goods are useful only if the appropriate equivalent is obtained for them. The use- value of goods is reflected in the properties of goods that satisfy human needs with their material characteristics, and the value of goods is a social determinant and is expressed in money or price. The current situation is such that the use-value of goods in our society is incomparably higher than its social value, expressed in money, ie in price. And that, it is believed, only at the local level. It is difficult to say anything about its price on a global level. At the global level, goods that have great use-value are devalued, undervalued, and degraded and their flow is restricted at the local level, so they cannot come or reach the global level.

Who came up with globalization, who needs it, why, and according to what criteria can restrictions be gradually lifted?

III – PEOPLE LIES AND EVIL

There are many paths. The only one is the fight against demons.

Evil is the imposition of political will, the imposition of one's will on others. Covert coercion or other means, including bribery. All this is to avoid the personal development of the individual.

Violence is the physical, psychological, and emotional abuse of someone you live with.

Health is protection from restlessness and insomnia.

This is the reason to be responsible for your actions.

Protect yourself and others from unwise moves.

Peace is doing things that don't hurt others.

Don't steal out of unrest, do not steal small things.

Peace is when you are not afraid.

Dignity is when you realize that you have done something unreasonable and then you can stop.

How do be incorruptible and benevolent, to have self- esteem and humor?

Problem 1:

How do you deal with what happens in your life?

Until a person decides to stop using the smoke screen, until he devotes himself much more deeply to solving problems from childhood symptoms, subjective experiences – harmful and useless psychological and physical signs will continue to torment him.

Everything is in a man's head. It seems that noting importance has changed in life.

What gender is the devil? Does he have a body? Is it some kind of energy? Is it, just, a concept? Did you make a contract with him?

Poetry confronts reality, however painful that reality may be.

Are you aware of your negative emotions? Anger, frustration, anxiety, depression, and, above all, sadness and grief?

Your thoughts, by themselves, are not able to control external events.

Problem 2: EVIL

Is evil, since time immemorial, in the center of attention, only, the religious thoughts of mankind?

Is it in the minds of science and psychology, in particular?

Religion and science are incompatible, they do not mix, and they reject each other. They made an unwritten non-binding agreement.

Is the world, really, arbitrarily divided into "natural" and "supernatural"? Is there a "supernatural"? Is "supernatural" really the sovereign territory of religion? Is religion itself "supernatural", when is its sovereign territory "supernatural"? Remind me what it was "belief".[6]

What is spirituality?

Spirituality is a state of mind in which a person pays attention to what is in his immediate environment. For example, dealing with philosophy or writing poetry.

The spirit is the inner essence of man, the totality of character, knowledge, and convictions. The spirit is also the overall character of a thing. For example the spirit of the era, the folk spirit, and the spirit of the times.

6   Belief is a directed, desired state, based on the subject's active belief in the truth of its content. Belief, as its subject, has some assertions. He has an affirmative attitude towards that statement, as opposed to ambiguity, disbelief in doubt, and other attitudes related to the statement. (Ž. V.)

45

Is it true that science has agreed not to stick its nose in anything spiritual? Is it true that science has agreed not to poke its nose into anything that has to do with the value system? Is it true that science has defined itself as „value-free" and that the answers to all these, previous, questions, weaknesses, and shortcomings of science are related to religion?

Is there a problem with evil?

The word evil represents evaluation, a priori. Science is free from evaluation. That is why science is not allowed to deal with the topics of evil, says religion.

Yes, by any chance, one important detail, an element, was not been deliberately omitted, obscured, or incorrectly stated here. This detail is that science has valued religion and determined its place in the systems of human knowledge. This clearly and unequivocally confirms that religion undermines science to define itself as "free from evaluation".

Are scientific approaches and methodologies, in general, reductionist? What and if they are? Do they work analytically, with the „left side of the brain"? What if they do? What about the "right side of the brain"? Is she more integrative? What if it is? What is the „right-brain" means of meditation, intuition, feeling, faith, and revelation? Why do poets use the "right side of the brain"? Which side of the brain is more useful? Left or right? Well, I'll stop here. We want to single out, as negative, two means from the "right side of the brain". These are faith and revelation. Faith is a subjective judgment about the truth of an assertion without its verification, that is, logical reasoning and conclusion. It is largely based on the belief that something is good, true, beautiful, or just. For deepening the knowledge and value of faith, the answer to the question, what do you believe in is important? That is why we answered that question earlier. Revelation is an illusion, a wrong, distorted perception of certain objects or phenomena, in reality, conditioned by some objective or subjective factors. As for the remaining tools from the "right side of the brain", meditation, intuition, and feelings, they are very positive and very useful to use, and, it is sincerely and from the heart recommend to man.

All in all, it is sincerely and from the heart, recommended to a person to use, as actively as possible, both the "left side of the brain" and the "right side of the brain", but, if at all possible, to leave out faith and revelation. These two concepts, in this study, were evaluated as negative for men.

Are good and evil mysteries? If there is no good, how would one know what evil is? Evil opposes living and life.

Life is a complex and active process of searching, selecting, receiving, processing, organizing, and interpreting various stimuli that affect the senses and nervous system. Life is mobility, consciousness, growth, autonomy, and will.

Healing is the result of love. Love for truth, for life, warmth, light, laughter, spontaneity, joy, help, and human care.

Who are the evil people? Why is the true self-image often different from the created self-image? You must have understanding and compassion for other people, primarily for yourself.

Evil people confuse us. We lose the ability to think. Lies are confusing. Evil people are people of lies. By lying to others, they also build layers of self-deception. There is no need to condemn them to hell. They are already in it. Their characteristic is not their sins, as such, but the concealment and persistence with which they commit them. Their fundamental flaw is not their sinfulness, but their refusal to admit it.

The understanding of evil is in the words "image", "appearance" and "outward".

There is a dilemma with evil people: they want to be good, but they have no motivation to be good.

Evil people take the law into their own hands when they destroy the life or vitality of the people around them, all in defense of the narcissistic image they have about themselves.

Nobody is born evil. Evil becomes gradual, over time, through a long series of wrong choices.

WHAT DOES ELIJAH THINK OF EVIL?

God and Jesus Christ are ideas, and concepts, created by bad thinkers, who dreamed that, with the help of these concepts, they would solve their problems. It remains unclear who these ad thinkers are and who is their ancestor? What are, all, the problems, that they thought they would solve? They noticed other people's troubles and problems, and they wanted to get rid of their troubles and problems. They didn't know how, so they blamed everything on the individual and his imperfections and wrong choices in life. God and Jesus Christ are hollow shadows on the earth, which, the worst dreamers, believe are solid ground. (Fernando Pessoa) Evil, inequality, and injustice still exist. They are the result of human life in a community with other people, living in society. There are social laws in society. They change and are different in different periods. Social laws are more complex than natural ones. One should understand and master social laws to create the conditions for prosperity.

Psychiatry is in trouble when it says: No one is born evil. Evil becomes gradual, over time, through a long series of wrong choices. Man's choices are not free. They are determined by the conditions in which a person lives, society, and the laws that govern society. Psychiatry has freed itself from the treatment of a sick society, and therefore from the consequences that a sick society has on the health of an individual in that society.

Psychiatry dared to say: That the healty is the easiest to treat because they are honest, and think honestly. It is the most difficult to treat the sick because they think dishonestly. What does psychiatry want? To get rid of the treatment of the sick, of everything that is sick? What if they are diagnosed with dishonest thoughts about the ill effects of their illness? Psychiatry suggests that man is to blame for his fate because his wrong choices are avoidance of responsibility for the treatment and health of the individual. This is an ominous departure from the definition of health, which is that health is not only the absence of disease but a state of complete psychophysical well- being. Psychiatrists, who, even when they turn to religion, absolve themselves of personal responsibility for the treatment of all people, regardless of race, nation, religion, or political belief. As we have seen, they simply freed themselves from the treatment of a sick society, rejected it, and fled. Adhering to a religion, psychiatrists introduce the religious value of judgment to triage people who are in treatment and those who are not. History knows that many evils arose and happened from religion, the imposition of religious will on other people, very sophisticated methods, and vulgar, as well as conflicts between different religions. In this way, psychiatry obscures the view of science and is destructive to itself. It obscures the view of society as a whole, of social laws, which lead people to inequality, injustice, and even disease, including psychiatric ones.

"He who does evil, defending himself from evil, does not do any evil." (P. P. Njegosh)

We have seen the pretension of religion that, supposedly, only religion, not science, deals with the question of evil. Isn't the above terse attempt to defend religion and an attempt to justify a religion by harming another religion, as well as an attempt to defend and justify this poet himself? Let's remember, religion has taken upon itself, only it deals with the problem of evil, and only it knows what evil is. And psychiatry deals with the problem of evil, only, and if it joins religion? Let us ignore, for now, the possible ambiguity of the verse and the time in which it was written.

GROUP AND LEADER DYNAMICS

Leaders become spontaneously and unconsciously. The reason is: that an individual is more capable or, at least, more willing than others to become one. The main reason: most people prefer to be guided. It is easier to be a follower than a leader. A follower does not have to bother with making complex decisions and planning, risk being unpopular, or stand out with courage. An adult is the individual master of his ship and the manager of his destiny. It is a misconception that leaders were chosen from among the members of the group. They are determined from higher levels, under various, often insufficiently clear influences, and shrouded in symbols of authority.

THE POINT

They are all hollow shadows on the earth, which, the worst dreamers, believe are solid ground. (Fernando Pessoa)

IV – METOH AND ME - a poem

In this new poetic inspiration, unstoppable, completely suggestive, and from an empathic experience, the poet, in the ecstasy of his emotional charge, without pause, cathartically exorcises his pain and thus gilds his poetic soul, which is, in that the existential position remained a lyricist, one who turns philosophical discourse into a lyrical tone.

The Antaeus complex and its varieties took the poet under their wing! When what happened happened, perhaps the most harmless thing is to heal his wound with poetry, which cannot be healed, but that's why poetry is the only one that can alleviate them!

I'm glad that Antaeus is Greek, which does not mean that the psychological phenomenon, which in science was called the Antaeus complex, is a universal human phenomenon!

Nature has taken care to prevent the wishies of globalization because this phenomenon is marked as the goal of modern civilization!

Medicine knows that the therapeutic mission of Antaeus is indisputable! Who knows how many lives he saved, those who were filled by that complex, to raise their lives to the point where that life could be

49

maintained and overcome the trauma that was inflicted on him, not through his fault, nor due to his merits. It is certain because experience has confirmed, that in the life of every person who lives, there are days and nights in which the past is renewed, most often as an emotional experience in dreams and visions, without which no living being belongs to the human species! We witness it on the spot, in the poem "METOH and ME"!

Jovan N. Striković

Is this, ferocious globalization, not subtly, but precociously sophisticated, forcing Todor to be a sad lyricist and his only inspiration for poetry being the sad songs of the Metohija's girls?

"Everything falls apart, only feelings remain."

KU-KLUX-KLAN IN PODGORICA

INTRODUCTION

KKK1 has the task of completing the job, which is in his competence. KKK3 is hired to perform this work. Indirectly, through his assistant, KKK1 informs the Negro by phone that KKK3 will come to him to finish the job.

I ACT

The Negro is sitting at the table, at his workplace.

KKK3 enters with two associates. The Negro gets up with a smile to make everything possible and depends on him for the KKK3 and his associates to finish the job. The distance between KKK3 and the Negro in the room where they met is about three meters. In that intermediate space is the table at which the head of the Service sits. KKK3 will not work. His reddened face popped out from under his ashen hair in an uncontrollable rage for some unknown reason. Caries appear instead of a front tooth. A slicked-back lock of his thin, gray hair flutters over his right ear. He provokes a heated argument and leaves the room together with his colleagues.

The Negro is sitting at his workplace, where he was sitting before the KKK3 entered the workplace.

The next day, the Negro receives a summons to the Disciplinary Commission, accused of allegedly wanting to physically deal with the KKK3.

The black man is shocked.

II ACT – DISCIPLINARY COMMISSION

Chaired by KKK2.

KKK1 is not visible. He is above. He pulls the strings that move the puppets in this puppet theater. You can't see his gray hair under the white hood, his flattened nose, or his stomack, which tightens his white mantle. He fell alone, he killed himself.

Assistant KKK1 is attending the trial. He carefully and meticulously follows every detail of the trial. She vividly brought into her role all the characteristics of a unique and inimitable monster that ever existed in the Microcosm. She zealously brought all these qualities into this KU–KLUX-KLAN.

Evidence is presented. KKK3 confirms the allegations in the indicment. The allegations from the indictment are confirmed by one of the associates of KKK3, whose number is unknown since the Ku– Klux– Klan is a very numerous organization. In his defense, the Negro says that he did not want to get a physical settlement with KKK3. President KKK2 delivers the verdict. The Negro is sentenced to death.

The fact that they did not kill him before is taken into account as a mitigating circumstance. Therefore, the execution of the judgment is postponed for one year, but if KKK1, during that period of one year, calls the Negro again with the help of his assistant, the verdict will be executed automatically.

III ACT

The Negro has a headache so he cannot sleep, and he has to go to work. He does not know what to do with himself. He signs up for a medical examination and treatment. The doctor sends him to the psychiatrist. The psychiatrist ask for laboratory findings, an X-ray scan of the spinal neck, and a CT scan of the brain. Based on these findings, a psychiatris diagnoses post- traumatic depression. The psychiatrist refers the Negro to a specialist in clinical psychology for psychotherapy. The Negro regulary goes to pscyhoterapy for a long time.

IV ACT – CONVERSATION

It is not known how the work, which was the responsibility of KKK1 and which should have been completed by KKK3, was completed. The essential element of this Ku Klux Klan drama remained obscured, unexplained, and unilluminated. Why did the KKK1, through his assistant, call a Negro on the phone to inform him that KKK3 would come to finish the announcement job?

The mentioned job was not the responsibility of the Negro and the Negro is not obligated or obliged to do it. Was it intense pressure from the KKK1, on a Negro, to force him to do a job that was not his responsibility? What did the KKK1 want?

It is important to emphasize that KKK2 was an extremely valuable member of his organization. He was bored with examining the vaginas of female patients in the Hospital. More than that, he liked to scratch for some self-governing position, even if it was the position of president of the Workers' Council. He had a distinct talent to be in contact with those "from above", so he knew, above all, whether the information coming from "above" was fresh or stale, and whether it was worth listening to or turning one's head, cover their ears so as not to hear.

FACES:

KKK1

KKK2

KKK3

Negro – an African-American, who happened to be in the Microcosm at the time, who has nothing to do with Elijah of Thunder, who was not born thirty-five years before that event at the institution, which is the forerunner of the same Clinical Hospital Center, and who does not live two kilometers away from the place of action, but, on the other side of Moraca.

PLACE:

Montenegro, Clinical Hospital Center Podgorica

TIME OF WORK:

1987 – The Ku-Klux-Klan Prohibition Act has not yet been introduced in the country

Reference: William Shakespeare

NDBiH

A country on the Balkan Peninsula. It borders Croatia, Serbia, and Montenegro. 21.2 km long, near Neum, it exits to the Adriatic Sea, until further notice. The capital, and largest, is Sarajevo. The official language is dejure - no, de facto - Bosnian, Croatian, and Serbian. Parliamentary constitutional, federal democratic republic. It consists of two entities: the Federation of Bosnia and Herzegovina and the Republika Srpska. Constituent peoples: Bosniaks, Croats, and Serbs. According to the 2013 census, it has 3,931,159 inhabitants.

The High Representative of the United Nations oversees and coordinates the implementation of the civilian aspects of the Dayton Accords, officially signed in Paris on 14 December 1995. The agreement ended the war in Bosnia from 1992 to 1995.

A FAST PASSAGE THROUGH THE HISTORY OF BIH

1154 - Banovina Bosna

1377 - Establishment of the Kingdom of Bosnia

1463 - Fall of the Kingdom of Bosnia under Ottoman rule At the time of their existence, the Banovina of Bosnia and the Kingdom of Bosnia were subordinated to the Croatian- Hungarian Kingdom. They were vassals of that kingdom.

1908 (October 7) - Annexation of Bosnia and Herzegovina to Austria-Hungary

1943 (November 25) - ZAVNOBiH

1992 (March 1) - Declaration of independence of BiH from SFRY. On the same day, the first victims fell and marked the beginning of the war in BiH.

1995 (November 21 agreed in Deyton, and signed in Paris on December 14) - Dayton Peace Agreement. The Dayton Accords were preceded by the NATO bombing of Republika Srpska from August 30 to September 20, 1995.

The conflicting parties were:

NATO (14 countries, led by the United States, including Turkey) against Republika Srpska. The cause of the bombing was: The Markale massacre of Sarajevo civilians. The result of the bombing was the cessation of the siege of Sarajevo, which was held by the Army of the Republika Srpska. According to the court rulings of the Hague Tribunal, the Republika Srpska Army is responsible for the two Markale Massacres. There are opinions of some experts from foreign countries that the massacres in Mar- kale were a provocation carried out by the Army of Bosnia and Herzegovina to provoke the intervention of NATO forces against the Army of Republika Srpska. Former UN special envoy Yatsushi Akashi and the United Nations Committee conducted their research. According to that research, the case remained unresolved.

THE OTTOMAN PERIOD OF POWER IN BiH IN BRIEF

In 1463, Sultan Muhammad II invaded Bosnia with 150,000 soldiers. In 1482, Herzegovina was conquered.

From 1463 to 1580, there were eight areas (sandžaks) on the territory of today's Bosnia and Herzegovina: Bosanski, Zvornik, Herzegovina, Klis, Požega, Lika, Pakrac, Bihać.

1580 - 1867. Bosnian pashaluk (ejalet)

1867 to 1908. Bosnian vilayet

ELIJAH OF THUNDER:

Why are you not, now, united with the Serbs, but one against the other?

NDBiH:

Because Serbs think that we are Turks, who nailed them to the stake for 500 years. They cannot understand that we are not Turks, but Bosniaks.

They want to take away Bosnia from us, even though we are natives, the oldest people in the Balkans and Europe.

PARADOX:

"There were no Croats or Serbs in Bosnia until the beginning of the 19th century."[7] In ancient times, peoples were named after the territory in which they lived. For example, Rome - Romans, Athens - Athenians, etc. In the 19th century, the territories began to be named after the people who live in them. So we have: Serbs - Serbia,

Croats - Croatia.

A paradox has occurred in Bosnia. The oldest name for the territory, in the Balkans, Bosnia, became the name for the newest people in the Balkans, Bosniaks, at the beginning of the last decade of the 20th century. Who will explain and solve this paradox? Of course, provided he does not watch, read and rewrite the end of the chapter

ELIJAH OF THUNDER AND NDBiH - PART II of this book.

"There is no historical continuity according to which any nation in present-day BiH would remain faithful to the pre- Ottoman cultural and civilizational heritage and at the same time retain Bosnian ethnic self-awareness."

The only motive for everyone was to defend the hearth, the doorstep, and the equality of their people. Apart from Bosnia, they had no other country. There were more of them than there was love in one song, now they are gone. The rest are wonderful even when they are not kissing. (Izet Sarajlic)

---

7   Example: The Petrovići, from whom the Petrović dynasty emerged in Montenegro, moved from the Njegoš mountain in Bosnia in the 17th century. At that time, in Bosnia, there was the Ottoman rule. They declared themselves as Serbs. „They didn't want to be chained."(P.P.Nj.) Hollow shadows on earth that those worst dreamers believe are solid ground. (F. P.) Out of Europe?

PARALLEL

1950 - May 9 - "Schuman Declaration" - a proposal to establish the European Coal and Steel Community, supranational institutions that will prevent further war between France and Germany, and the integration of industry, which was important for the war.

1951 - April 18 - The European Coal and Steel Community is formed. The ultimate goal is the creation of a European federation. The unification of the nations of Europe requires the removal of the ancient enmity between France and Germany

1952 - Born Elijah Of Thunder.

1957 - Treaties of Rome. EEC – European Economic Community and Euratom formed.

1987 - September 24 - Eighth session of the Central Committee of the League of Communists of Serbia. It determined the direction that Serbia will take for the next 13 years. She started the so-called Anti-bureaucratic revolution.

Practically at the same time, that autumn, the KU-KLUKS- KLAN in Podgorica sentenced a black man to death but postponed the execution of his sentence for a year. The verdict will be executed automatically when, for the first time after the verdict is pronounced, the KKK1 aide calls the Negro by phone.

1989 - At the beginning of the year - Completed the so- called. Anti-bureaucratic revolution. It overthrew the provincial authorities of Vojvodina and Kosovo and the republican authorities in Montenegro. In that way, Serbia gained control of the federal presidency and the League of Communists of Yugoslavia.

1989 – June 28 - Slobodan Milosevic's speech in Gazimestan, on the occasion of the 600th anniversary of the Battle of Kosovo.

1989 - November 9 - Fall of the Berlin Wall.

During 1989, revolutions took place in six Eastern Bloc countries: Poland, Hungary, East Germany, Bulgaria, Czech- Slovakia, and Romania. One-party, communist political systems were destroyed and multi-party political systems were switched.

1989 - December - Ante Markovic's expositions in the SFRY Assembly: We will pay dearly for misconceptions about poverty, poisoning of the spirit, and the position of the distant periphery of Europe.

1990 - January 22 - 14th Extraordinary Congress of the League of Communists of Yugoslavia at the Sava Congress Center in Belgrade. The delegations of the League of Communists of Slovenia and Croatia left the session. They did not want the new leadership from Serbia to impose its will on them. Vinko Hafner had previously, on time, with his finger raised, publicly warned the Leader of the delegation of the Serbian Sports Confederation to be careful which way he would go, because he leads the most numerous people in Yugoslavia. Did Europe know Yugoslavia better than Yugoslavia knew itself? Thus, the SKJ was dissolved, and it ceased to exist.

1990 - March 1 – The collapse of the USSR begins.

1990 - October 3 - United Germany.

1990 - Autumn - Illegal arming of Croatia for the needs of the Croatian Democratic Union and members of the Croatian Ministry of the Interior. This operation took place in strict secrecy and away from the public eye because the leadership of the FR of Croatia (Government, Parliament, and Presidency) was preparing for war, ie for a showdown with Serbs and members of the JNA in Croatia? Is this considered one of the key events in the break-up of Yugoslavia? (Source: Wikipedia.)

1990 - December 22 - Christmas Constitution of the Republic of Croatia. Croatia is defined as a sovereign and unified state with a democratic order and guaranteed political rights and human rights of all its citizens.

1991 - January 25 - Several members of the HDZ, who took part in an illegal weapons operation, are arrested. On May 20, they were convicted of armed rebellion and hostile action.

1991 - June 25 - Slovenia and Croatia declare independence from the SFRY.

1991 - August 27 - The EEC Council of Ministers forms the Badinter Commission, composed of 5 members, and presidents of the

EEC Constitutional Courts, whose task was to resolve disputed legal issues and speed up a peaceful solution to the crisis in the SFRY.

1991 - September 8 - Macedonia declares independence. 1991 - November 20 - Badinter Commission concludes that the SFRY is in the process of disintegration.

1991 - December 20 - Ante Markovic explains his resignation as federal prime minister: I have always been consistently in favor of democracy, peace, and against war. Therefore, for me, it is unacceptable to propose a war budget and I cannot and will not do that.8 (Why, did Borisav Jović, say that Ante is a hochstapler?)

1991 - December 26 - The collapse of the USSR is completed.

1992 - January 11 - Badinter Commission: - The Serb population in BiH and Croatia has all the rights related to minorities and ethnic groups. Republics must afford, to members of these minorities and ethnic groups, all human rights and freedoms recognized in international law, including, where possible, the choice of their nationality. The principle of Uti presidents applies

- everyone keeps what they currently keep under military control.

- The borders between Croatia and Serbia, BiH and Serbia, and possibly other neighboring independent states cannot be changed, except with a freely reached agreement. Unless otherwise agreed upon, former borders become borders protected by international law.

- The independence of BiH, at that time, should not be recognized, because it has not yet held an independence referendum.

- Croatia's independence should not be recognized because the Croatian Constitution did not include the protection of minorities required by the EC. Croatian President Tudjman assures Badinter that this shortcoming will be remedied. Based on this belief, the EC recognizes Croatia. Franjo Tudjman had no conversation or agreement with Helmut Kohl before he gave it to Badinter, your assurance that the Croatian Constitution, will protect the rights of minorities required by the EC? Are Helmut Kohl and Badinter out of Europe? Helmut Kohl did not exercise, with Badinter, the right to recognize the independence of Croatia at Francis' word?

- It is recommended that Macedonia's request for recognition be accepted.

- It is recommended to recognize Slovenia.

- DECISION: The legal process of disintegration of the SFRY is over. The SFRY no longer exists.

- The legal successors of the SFRY are all the successor states, with the correct division of international funds and obligations of the former SFRY.

- The FRY cannot legally become a continuation of the SFRY. The same criteria should be applied for the recognition of the FRY as for other states that emerged from the SFRY.

1992 - January 21 - The BiH Parliament decides to call a referendum.

1992 - January 31 - Bulgaria recognizes independent BiH. 1992 - February 6 - Turkey recognizes independent BiH.

Bulgaria and Turkey did not wait for the referendum to be called and its results. Are they non-aligned? Uninvolved? They had no idea what was happening and what was going on in the Balkans? Out of Europe? They never heard, nor did they know that, once upon a time, some 1912/13. years, some Balkan wars were fought, and that someone, for some reason, took part in those wars?

1992 - February 7 - Maastricht Treaty on European Union.

1992 - February 29 and March 1 - A referendum was called on the independence of BiH from the SFRY. Independence from the non-existent state of SFRY? Who created the legal basis for such a statement? Was it done according to this principle: first we will decide that it does not exist, and then you declare that you are independent of it, which we have decided not to exist?

1992 - March 1 - Declaration of independence of FR Bosnia and Herzegovina from SFRY. ON THE SAME DAY WHEN INDEPENDENCE WAS DECLARED, THE WAR IN BiH

BEGUN. For now, the war has four names: the Civil War in BiH, the Defense and Patriotic War (for the Serbs of RS), the Aggression against BiH (for Bosniaks in BiH), and the Homeland War (for Croats in BiH).

Cause of war: Separation of BiH from the SFRY.

Conflicting parties in the war:

The Republic of BiH, Croatia, and the Croatian Community of Herceg Bosna against the Republika Srpska, the SFRY, and the Republika Srpska Krajina.

How can the cause of the war be the secession of BiH from the SFRY, when the Badinter Commission previously decided that the SFRY does not exist and did not recognize BiH? Separation from the non-existent state?! Does this sequence of events indicate that the cause of the war is only the declaration and proclamation of independence of BiH? How can SFRY be a conflicting party ina a war when it ceased to exist before that?

1992 - April 6 - The European Union recognizes the NDBiH.

1992 - April 8 - The Croatian Defense Council is formed.

1992 - April 15 - BiH Army formed in Sarajevo.

1992 - April 27 - By the decision of the Assembly of the SFRY, the FRY was proclaimed. The SFRY ceased to exist.

How can the Assembly of the SFRY decide, when it was previously decided that the SFRY does not exist? How can the Parliament of a non-existed state be audited?

1992 - May 12 - The Army of the Republika Srpska is formed in Palam, Bijeljina and Banja Luka.

1992 - May 15 - The UN Security Council demands that all forms of external JNA interference in BiH be stopped immediately, that JNA units be withdrawn, brought under the control of the republican government, or disbanded and disarmed.

1992 - May 20 - Dissolved JNA, proclaimed VJ.

1992 - May 30 - The UN Security Council imposes sanctions on the FRY, ie Serbia and Montenegro, on charges of participating in the war in BiH. Security Council Resolution 757 provided for a complete international economic embargo on the FRY. It was assessed that the FRY was directly involved in the conflict in BiH. These were the most severe punitive measures the UN has ever taken against a country. The FRY was followed by a major economic crisis, hyperinflation, rising crime, and, in particular, smuggling.

1992 - December 1-31 – Elijah Of Thunder was "absent" from work in the Microcosm. The consequence of that absence was that he lost his job and source of personal income in the Microcosmos in March 1993 as well as social protection. The protagonists of this work are Escaped Spy from Bosnia, Anemic Director Hippocrates, Hepatobiliary Surgeon, and Tall Man Who Sees Highly Through The Microcosm. These four literary figures found themselves, illegally and irrelevantly, phantasmagorically, in this place, to be the pillars that hold the construction of the new

Microcosm, which has not yet been born. It will take a full fifteen years to be born. They didn't need bio-medical engineering, nor electronics, nor whether Elijah should work, as well as those pillars them. How will they need it when they were not yet born with the Microcosm, which they held and supported. In addition, the Identity of the Microcosm was not recognized. This will be officially achieved on October 19, 2007.

1992 to 1994 - The Republic of BiH, the Republic of Herceg-Bosna and Croatia against the Republika Srpska, the Republika Srpska Krajina, the AP of Western Bosnia, supported by the FRY.

Elijah Of Thunder, under the auspices of the United Nations High Commissioner for Refugees, is working to take care of refugees in the Microcosm.

1993 - November 1 - The Maastricht Treaty enters into force. THE EUROPEAN UNION has become a new political entity.

1994 to 1995 - The Republic of BiH, Croatia, and NATO against the Republika Srpska, the Republika Srpska Krajina, the AP of Western Bosnia, supported by the FRY.

1995 - August 30 to September 20 - NATO bombing of Republika Srpska.

1995 - December 14 - The Dayton Peace Agreement is signed in Paris and:

"When you shatter the head of the body, the limbs die in agony."
(P.P.Njegosh)

POWER, AUTHORITY, AND WAR

"The character of the man is the result of antagonisms in society." - Marx
"Antagonisms in human character produce antagonisms in society."- Freud
How to increase power? What good is power if he has no authority? !!!!!

Let's start with January 28, 1990, when he failed to increase his power and authority with the consent of the delegations of Slovenia and Croatia, at the Sava Center in Belgrade. The day when Vinko Hafner, with his raised finger, warned him to be careful which way he was going because he was leading the most numerous nation in Yugoslavia.

JASMIN KONDIĆ[8]:

The provisions of Article 72 of the Constitution of the Republic of Serbia, dated 28 September 1990, are contrary to the provisions of the Constitution of the SFRY. They usurp the three basic competencies of the federation in international relations, national defense, and state security.

Much more important than that is that, by the provision of Article 135, paragraph 2, Serbia is excluded from the legal system of the SFRY, because it envisages that it will "respect" federal laws only when it is in its interest.

This Constitution is separatist, adopted a year before the declaration of independence of Slovenia and Croatia.

With the provision from Article 72, the Republic of Serbia ceases to be part of the federation. It is an independent state and has no duties to the federation, of which it is no longer a member.

On the other hand, with the provision of Article 135 of the Constitution, independent Serbia, which has no duties to the federation,

---

8   Jasmin Kondić read the working version of this text and said: I think it would be best to meet with many other authors who write about it, and agree to write, as a group of authors, a multi-volume "encyclopedia" about everything that took place in the period from 1980 until today.

wants to retain the rights it once had, as a member of the federation. These rights are 1. participation in the work of the presidency of the state, to which it no longer belongs, 2. to maintain its control over the army through it, 3. to hide behind the name of Yugoslavia and advocate for the territorial integrity of Yugoslavia, 4. Claims a share of the federal treasury.

So, the independent Republic of Serbia has a claim, deprived of any legal basis, to continue to exercise the rights that once belonged to it, as a member of the federation and after it was constituted as an independent state, without due obligations towards the SFRY.

Why did the other republics agree to such a situation in which Serbia "exercises its rights" in a federation in which it has no obligations and to which it does not belong?

This can only be understood by the fact that Serbia has already controlled the Army and constantly threatened it. Fear of this threat and the desire to somehow avoid an armed conflict.

At the same time, this independent state "within the SFRY" manages to break into the monetary system of another country (SFRY) and voluntarily "borrows" from its primary issue of 1.4 billion dollars.

Following its status, the Republic of Serbia enacts its laws governing relations, which were once the responsibility of the federation. Duties are being introduced on goods from the republics of SFRY and other things that would be impossible according to the provisions of the Constitution of SFRY.

By declaring that it is "part of the SFRY", Serbia is merely expressing its will to unjustifiably exercise, in another state, some rights that no longer belong to it, as an independent state. Because Serbia, according to its own Constitution and behavior, is an independent state, the SFRY no longer exists, because it is a federation that lost the opportunity to exercise its sovereign rights on 41% of its territory and over 29% of the citizens of SFRY.

Other republics feared aggressive nationalist Serbia and the JNA. The power of "independent and sovereign" Serbia to impose itself on another state was thus based solely on threats of the use of force, which others rightly judged to be real. Forcing him to participate in the decisions of the "rest" of the federal bodies of the SFRY was a pure act of violence.

All in all, the SFRY ceased to exist on September 28, 1990, when Serbia was constituted as "sovereign and independent".

SLOBODAN MILOSEVIC, Hotel Grand - Cetinje

None of the five of us (Franjo Tudjman, Milan Kucan, Alija Izetbegović, Momir Bulatović, and He) have no mandate for breaking up Yugoslavia. And what do those five have mandate for?

QUESTIONS TO JASMIN KONDIĆ:

How can the cause of the war in Bosnia and Herzegovina be the secession from the SFRY, if the SFRY ceased to exist on September 28, 1990, with the adoption of the Serbian Constitution, and the legal process of dissolution of the SFRY ended on January 11, 1992, with decision of the Badinter Commission?

Was the war in Bosnia and Herzegovina a civil war or an interstate war? Who introduces this dilemma? Which of the two is true?

On June 25, 1991, two great territories and two peoples separated, which He hoped to have, to impose His power and authority. This separation passed with human casualties and destruction.

On March 1, 1992, another separation of territory and people began, which He hoped would have, that he will impose his power and his authority on them. This separation lasted longer than the previous one and with greater human casualties and destruction. His real power and authority slowly and with difficulty gained its true measure.

In 1996, where, it seems, there had long been "something rotten in the state of Denmark", something that the "state of Den- mark" could not or did not want or could not heal, began to flare up.

Time: April 22, 1996, to June 10, 1999

Place: Kosovo and Metohija, Serbia, FR Yugoslavia

Event: War

Cause: Albanian separatism

Conflicting sides:

FR Yugoslavia v. KLA (Kosovo Liberation Army), FARK (Format e Armatosura të Republikës së Kosovës - "Armed Forces of the Republic of Kosovo"), Mujahideen and NATO

1999 - March 24 to June 10 – NATO bombing of FR Yugoslavia

Conflicting sides:

The FRY versus NATO, led by the United States and 21 of Europe's largest and most modern countries, including Canada and Turkey.

The result:

Serbia was destroyed and razed to the ground. Under the Kumanovo Agreement and Resolution 1244, the Yugoslav Army and the Serbian Police withdrew from Kosovo and Metohija. The province became a protectorate of the United Nations within the FRY.

The anger and fury of the protectors must have been so great and unbearable because, in Serbia, there was not as much coal and steel as they needed.

Victims and losses:

About 1,000 dead on the FRY side.

About 4,000 dead guerrillas were on the side of the separatists and their allies.

2006 - June 3 - The Montenegrin Parliament adopts the Decision on Independence, which, after 88 years, makes Montenegro an independent state again.

2008 - February 17 - The Assembly of Kosovo unilaterally declared the independence of the Autonomous Province of Kosovo and Metohija from Serbia, creating the Republic of Kosovo.

SOUTHERN SLAVES AND UNIFICATION[9]

INTRODUCTION

Action time:

From the last decade of the 18th century to the last decade of the 20th century and the present.

Location:

The Western Balkans and the touching north-western region towards the rest of Europe.

Empires:

Austrian, Ottoman, Austro-Hungarian.

South Slavs: Underground.

Montenegro:

Four nahijas. Nahija is the smallest administrative unit in the Ottoman Empire (several villages). Larger administrative units are kaza, sandzak, and pashaluk (vilayet). Due to the inability to pay taxes, the population was declared free cattle breeders, and Montenegro had a special autonomy with the only obligation to guard the border with the Venetian Republic.

ACT I

The Sandzak-bey of Skadar is organizing military campaigns in Montenegro, which is his sub-area, to gain benefit for the Imperial government through violence and looting.

1786 - July 11 (according to the old calendar) Battle of Martinići. The Montenegrins, led by Peter I Petrovic Njegos, defeated the army led by Mahmud-pasha Bushatlija, the Sandzak-beg of the Skadar Sandzak.

---

9   Austrian Empire, Ottoman Empire, and Austro-Hungary.

1786 - September 22 (according to the old calendar) Battle of Krusi. The Montenegrins, again, defeated the army, led by Mahmud-pasha Bushatlija.

The Austrian Emperor helped the Montenegrins to win these battles by supplying them with weapons, gunpowder, lead, and other war equipment.

These battles are also considered heralds of the beginning of the end of the Ottoman Empire in the Balkans.[10]

MOSAIC - ROUND I

1804 - February 14 - The first Serbian uprising against the Ottoman Empire, led by Karadjordj.

1805 - December 26 - Peace of Požuna, signed in Bratislava, between France and Austria. Austria had to cede the Croatian coast to France: Istria, Dalmatia, and the Bay of Kotor.

1808 - The first grammar of the Slavic language, Jernej Kopitar, is published.

1813 - Oct. 7 - The downfall of the First Serbian Uprising.

1813 - October 29 - The Assembly of Montenegrins and Boka proclaims the unification of Montenegro and Boka.

1815 - April 23 - Second Serbian Uprising against the Ottoman Empire.

- from September 1 to June 9 - the Congress of Vienna: The Bay of Kotor became part of the Kingdom of Dalmatia, under Austrian rule, but not united with the rest of Croatia.

1817 - July 26 - Serbian victory in the Second Serbian Uprising and the founding of the Principality of Serbia.

1830 - Slovenia: The rejected ideology of common language with other South Slavs.

- Croatia: Croatian National Revival Begins.

---

10   Elijah of Thunder notes that Petar I Petrović Njegosh is a descendant of people who, according to family tradition, immigrated to Montenegro from Bosnia, where they could not be Montenegrins. He did not find any data that is more reliable than that family tradition. This observation contradicts the claims that there were no Serbs in the battles on Martinići and Krusi. The nation is a term that crystallized in the 19th century, after these battles. Nationalism is the source of everyone's evil. "They did not want to be bound in chains."

- Serbia: The Sultan gives a hatisherif, which confirms the self-governing rights of the Principality of Serbia, with the obligation to pay the annual tribute to the Porte. Serbia has a vassal relationship with the Ottoman Empire.

1831 - Montenegro: The Montenegrin and Mountain Governing Senate is established, the supreme provincial government in Montenegro.

1832 - Montenegro: Governorship abolished, secular political title oriented towards the Venetian Republic and Austria, captain's courts introduced.

- Bosnia and Herzegovina: The great Bosnian uprising of Bosnian feudal lords (Ayans, Agas, and Beys), led by the Dragon of Bosnia, for the autonomy of Bosnia within the Ottoman Empire. The insurgents fought to preserve the privileges that Sultan Mehmed II wanted to revoke through reforms in the Empire. 1834 - Montenegro: A printing house and a school are founded in Cetinje. 1835 - The first Constitution of Serbia.

1842 – The borders between Montenegro and the Austrian Empire are established.

1844 - Serbia: Draft of Ilija Garashanin. It outlines the elements of mutual acquaintance and rapprochement of the South Slavic peoples. The Serbian government is establishing ties and relations with the southern Slavs in Bosnia and Herzegovina, Montenegro, and Macedonia, and is trying to bring them together.

1847 - Croatia: Croatian becomes the official language in Croatia.

1848 and 1849 - Revolution in Europe. The Slovenes seek the unification of all the countries inhabited by the Slovenes within the Austrian Empire. The unification of the South Slavic peoples within the Austro-Hungarian Monarchy is constantly demanded.

They do not envisage leaving the Monarchy and going to the Balkans, to a distant European periphery. The Croatian Parliament adopted the request and demanded a confederate reorganization of the Monarchy, by uniting Slovenia, Croatia, and Serbian Vojvodina. This is the so-called South Slavic / Austrian political program. At the same time and in parallel with it, there is the Yugoslav / Balkan political program, which the Serbian government has harmonized with the Serbian national program.

MOSAIC - ROUND II

1850 - March 28 to April 3 - Vienna Literary Treaty. The historical agreement laid the foundations for the common Serbo-Croatian language. The Austrian Empire needed official political and legal terminology for the Slavic peoples of the Austrian Empire. The Ministry of the Monarchy financed this work, and the fruit of this work facilitated understanding of legal matters in the Slavic south and saved the administrative costs of translating foreign languages and dialects.

1852 - Montenegro: Danilo Petrović is proclaimed prince.

- Bosnia and Herzegovina: Omer-pasha Latas, cruelly and efficiently, implements the Sultan's reforms. He simply killed the ayans, the heads of local governments in the Bosnian pashaluc. Thus, with strong chains, he tied the Bosnian pashaluk to the central government in Constantinople.

1852, 1857, 1858, 1862 - Peasant uprisings in Bosnia and Herzegovina, due to the great obligations imposed on them by Ottoman rule. It is written somewhere that all these uprisings were aimed at expanding Serbia and Montenegro to Bosnia and Herzegovina.

1860 - Slovenia: Slogaštvo-Stilizam. Requirements for a United Slovenia with administration in Slovene and teaching in primary and secondary schools in Slovene, not German.

1867 - Serbia: Sultan's decree (firman) on the withdrawal of the Turkish army from Serbia.

1868 - Croatian-Hungarian settlement. Hungary recognized the Kingdom of Croatia as a political nation and territorial integrity, but it was subordinate to Hungary.

1876 - Montenegrin army captures Niksic, Bar and Ulcinj.

1878 - June 13 - July 13 - Berlin Congress:

    - Recognized independence of Montenegro and Serbia.

    - Austro-Hungary gained the right to occupy Bosnia and Herzegovina.

1878 - July 27 - Bosnians establish the National Committee and the National Assembly (12 Muslims, 5 Orthodox, 2 Catholics, and 1 Jew), overthrow the Ottoman government in Sarajevo, and organize resistance to the Austro-Hungarian occupation. The resistance was crushed after three months of fighting.

1882 - March 7 - Serbia has proclaimed a Kingdom.

In the 19th century, the South Slavic peoples did nothing in the field of creating a common South Slavic culture, gathering around common institutions and projects in the field of language, culture, economy, political program, political community, political institutions, journalism, education, etc. The process is such that it can only be understood as from direct (individual) to general and common multinational South Slavism, and that it should be realized on the principle of federal pluralism.

MOSAIC - ROUND III

1905 - December 19 - St. Nicholas Constitution. Prince Ni- kola enacted (imposed) the Constitution.

1908 - October 5 - Austro-Hungary turns the occupation of Bosnia and Herzegovina into annexation. This ended Ottoman rule in Bosnia and Herzegovina.

1910 - Montenegro has proclaimed a Kingdom.

By analyzing such chronologically arranged events and circles of mosaics, as they are listed on the Internet and in the cited scientific literature, it is not possible to find:

1. That, in the 19th century, cultural, political, and emancipatory movements took place in Bosnia and Herzegovina, or were felt, and especially not initiated, which, at that time, took place in Europe and in the nations where Sout Slavic an idea, not even a national individuality, that developed among the nearest neighbors. In the absence of a joint program of Yugoslav policy with Serbia, Croatian politicians have, since 1878, sought to join Bosnia and Herzegovina in the South Slavic confederation within Austria-Hungary. Supplementing or refuting this finding is welcome.

2. From 19th-century Macedonia, it was practically the same as said above for Bosnia and Herzegovina. Without her initiative for a joint South Slavic initiative, national specificity and identity developed. But the 19th century has passed, and so has the 20th. Something short, fast, and leaps and bounds about that 20th century.

The first joint Yugoslav political program and, to some extent, the possibility of its realization, appeared only during the First World War.

STATE OF SERBS, CROATS, AND SLOVENS

1918 - October 28 - The Croatian Parliament severed all state and legal ties with Austro-Hungary and formed a state, from the countries of the former Austro-Hungary, where the South Slavic peoples lived.

73

The Entente powers, Russia, France, and the United Kingdom have not recognized the country.

from 6 to 9 November - The Geneva Declaration stipulates that the State of SCS and the Kingdom of Serbia, as two equal partners, establish a joint South Slavic state, the internal organization of which will be decided by the Constituent Assembly, elected on democratic principles. Thus the Slovenci, Croats, and Serbs from Austria-Hungary joined the winners of the First World War. Bosniaks are not mentioned in that declaration, so it is not clear which side they are on.

The Kingdom of Serbs, Croats, and Slovenes was created.

Thus, finally, that day came, to solve real, long-awaited problems. The Geneva Conference gave instructions and a recipe for how to solve everything in the best way.

That's how it would be if we didn't know what it was and how it was.

INSTEAD OF CONCLUSIONS
- Let's remind ourselves -

In the First World War, Germany and France were opposed to each other. France and its allies won.

In the Second World War, the scenario was repeated, which, in a way, was similar to the outcome of the First World War. Germany was defeated, and France, again with its allies, was victorious.

Robert Schumann was a German by birth, a lawyer by education, and later a prominent French politician and minister. He was both French and German.

He experienced the troubles and sufferings of the First and Second World Wars. In 1950, as the minister of France, he suggested how to achieve that France and Germany no longer go to war with each other, to overcome their traditional enmity. He suggested that France and Germany be connected and brought closer by utilizing a common resource, a common interest, namely coal, and steel. To form a supranational body. The European Community for Coal and Steel to manage this wealth and distribute the profits. (Middle of the 20th century: something is needed outside the nation as well!) Profit primarily to France and Germany, and then, a little, to others, who find own interest in their profit. There must be no more war between France and Germany. Whether others will go to war is a separate question and a separate story. Let everyone hold on to their coal and steel. They mustn't get close to French and German coal and steel.

And so it would. France and Germany have not been at war since 1945. That is already 73 years.

These others? Remember.

Imperialism is the highest stage in the development of capitalism or the last Chinese emperor and the cultural revolution?

What did the South Slavs do? In the 19th century, Slovenians and Croats were looking for ways and answers to resist the hegemony of other peoples with whom they lived in the same state. In the 20th Century, they saw the benefits of living together with other "Southern brothers". They chose and found a way to separate themselves from them and get closer to those they wanted to resist in the 19th century. They believe that the other "Southern brothers" should follow them, as they know and are able, and if they know and can.

Globalization is the goal of modern civilization. National states - small states resemble pens, from which something needs to be taken, and, one would say, there is nothing to take. The resources of small nation-states, practically, have not changed and cannot, practically, but there is still profit and someone is reaping it. While the South Slavs, in the 20th century, did what they did and thought they were smart, the French and Germans combined their coal and steel (raw materials) and, in peace, came to the epicenter of the EU. Southern Slavs, almost all of them, can take pictures and get their feet wet in the nearby stream.

Is the correct answer: In this round, the EU won?

"If there was no French hill, the Arabian Sea would sink everything."

Appendix
MIRJANA KULJAK[11]

ELIJAH OF THUNDER (ET): I am interested in the exact number of South Slavic nations is and who are they?

MIRJANA KULJAK (MK): Topic for googling and discussion. Who is in the mood, I have no time...

ET: I was afraid that another South Slavic people would appear, who would want to unite them ...

REPRESENTATIVE MK: There are 7 South Slavic nations. Bulgarians, Macedonians, Serbs, Montenegrins, Bosnians, Croats, Slovenes. YU itself had 6 peoples, two nationalities, and one nation.[12] But most do not know the difference between a people, a nationality, and a nation.

ET: What is the difference between a people (not a nationality) and a nation?

REPRESENTATIVE MK: The difference is in the level of development. The peoples belong to the pre-industrial era. They are the population of feudal states. Nations, ie. Civil communities have been created since the French bourgeois revolution. The bourgeoisie wanted one market, the right to vote, and the national languages for the official ones. It is a new group, a subject. The people are not the subject, the tribe is.[13] The tribe does not have a state or a letter. The people have a state and a letter, but they don't ask. A nation has a state, an alphabet, its official language, and it is asked.

11   Source: https://www.facebook.com/mirjana.kuljak
12   The answer here is incomplete. Which are these two nationalities and which is one nation? We accept, as correct, the answer that one ethnic group was Albanian. Which is another and which is one nation?
13   Why are you talking about a tribe, when it comes to the difference between the people and a nation?

The Germans / Nation originated from more than 30 peoples (Bavarians, Prussians, Saxons, Swabians...), arising from Germanic tribes. Do you understand now?

Our problem is that we are in rural consciousness and at that level, the identity is primarily religious. European nations, when are emerging, are following the process of secularization, and for us, the clergy is forcing YU, Strossmayer, and Njegosh. Simply, in our country, the sea is from the roof and by force, and such houses are being demolished.[14]

ET: That's not true! YU did not forced by the clergy! If someone forced it, then he chose the smartest people of that time, to create it. You and me are not on rural consciousness, nor religious. Do you notice that you said: Germans are a nation, born of several peoples. In our country, the South Slavs, the process is reversed: several nations are created from one, that is, seven nations. Isn't that a paradox? Why is that so? Is the Balkans the front yard of Europe?

---

14 This claim is problematic. You don't have to do anything. Based on this, it is logically concluded that it is not easy. Why, in our country, do you have to do it from the roof and by force, when you don't have to do anything?

ELIJAH OF THUNDER AND THE SHOCKING HISTORICAL TRUTH

ELIJAH OF THUNDER:

What is the cause of the disintegration of Yugoslavia?

SHOCKING HISTORICAL TRUTH:

The creation of Yugoslavia is the cause of the disintegration of Yugoslavia.

ELIJAH OF THUNDER:

Who created Yugoslavia and why?

SHOCKING HISTORICAL TRUTH:

It was created by the Great Powers for their interests?

ELIJAH OF THUNDER:

Did they tear it apart?

SHOCKING HISTORICAL TRUTH:

It is said that Slobo and Momir did it.

ELIJAH OF THUNDER:

Do not say that: "it is said" and "she said - she said", but as historical science says.

SHOCKING HISTORICAL TRUTH:

Fraternal Serbia led Montenegro to war. Those two have been doing shit for 10 years.

ELIJAH OF THUNDER:

I fully accept your answer that the creation of Yugoslavia is the cause of its disintegration. Based on that answer, it is concluded that it should not have been created. Let us repeat: it was created by the Great Powers for their interests. Precise question: Who dismembered?

SHOCKING HISTORICAL TRUTH:

SANU, Momir, and Slobodan are the main culprits.

ELIJAH OF THUNDER:

Is it possible that those three are so and so big simpletons? What are they guilty of, when you say that they did not create Yugoslavia, nor they are the cause of its disintegration?

SHOCKING HISTORICAL TRUTH:

For 200 years, it was almost the preparation of the history of Greater Serbia from 1804 to the present day.

ELIJAH OF THUNDER:

In 1804, there was the First Serbian Uprising against Turkey, the Ottoman government in the so-called to the Belgrade pashaluk, and it was the Smederevo pashaluk.

Who and how prepared 200 years of history contrary to the history of Greater Serbia, from 1804 to the present day?

SHOCKING HISTORICAL TRUTH:

One is an idea and the other is implementation. Do not be lost in the nonsense of historical reality.

ELIJAH OF THUNDER:

That's why I'm talking to you. Do you want to answer the previous question and tell me who, for 200 years, from 1804. to the present day, prepared a opposite history of the history Greater Serbia?

SHOCKING HISTORICAL TRUTH:

This has been the case for you since the beginning of time and it will not change. Take it this way: people are perishable goods, when they see that they can or think they can, they will hit you. SANU, together with Momir and Slobodan, has done this to all other nations ex yu, and there are countless such examples throughout history.

ELIJAH OF THUNDER:

Can you tell me what happened to JAZU, or HAZU, as it is now called? Didn't those academies cooperate? All academies in the world cooperate. It is an integral part of their work and name. It's called inter-academic cooperation ... Do you remember Bogdan Bogdanovic? He said SANU is a home for the elderly where a valid debate cannot be heard. He packed his bags and left, fleeing to Vienna. He was the mayor of Belgrade.

SHOCKING HISTORICAL TRUTH:

You have to read a lot about the history of the South Slavs, I see.

ELIJAH OF THUNDER:

You know, I don't have time to deal with the history of the South Slavs. I'm from a completely different field, but it's interesting to me because I see that you know history very well. Here, through a conversation with you, for the first time in my life, I learned that there was a state called the "Triune Kingdom of Croatia, Slavonia, and Dalmatia". I had no idea about it. The same is true, for example, of the history of Austria or Austria-Hungary. I didn't study in school, I studied another field, and my hobby didn't draw me to those topics.

Serbia to Tokyo, Croatia to the Drina, Bosnia to Istanbul, Montenegro to Milan, and I need to develop a polycentric consciousness as if watching a drama in a theater!

I should have a divergent mode of explaining socio-historical processes.!?!!!

Help! It is about the crust of bread, science, culture, education, and professionalism.

"I'm sick and tired of repeating myself." - History.

SHOCKING HISTORICAL TRUTH ABOUT GENOCIDE AGAINST BOSNIAKS

Ms. NDBiH's story should be viewed in the context of Bosniak ideology, ie Islamic fundamentalism. In all these places, in Serbia, Slavonia, Dalmatia, Montenegro, and Kosovo, were Bosniaks Muslims, or, mostly, the local population, who accepted Islam? Bosniaks are Bosnians who have embraced Islam. Their relationship with Turkey is primarily religious and cultural. It is interesting and significant, that, when, 200 years ago, the Ottoman Empire weakened and accepted Western customs, in Bosnia they refused with indignation because they were the border eyalet, which, now and then, fought against Austria and, earlier, the Venetians. The Sultan often calculated with Bosnia, and in Bosnia, he had people willing to fight for him.

Ms. NDBiH, unjustifiably, appropriates the Muslim population of other areas of the Balkans asBosniaks. He equates, confuses, and interprets anachronistic terms: Bosniak, Muslim, and Turkish.

As far as genocide is concerned, Ms. NDBiH is right when she says that everything started with Austria and Venice, and continued with Serbia, Njegosh, and certain influences from the West, such as Gladstone and his pamphlets.

AFTERWORD

„There is no historical continuity according to which any nation in present-day BiH would remain faithful to the pre- Ottoman cultural and civilizational heritage while maintaining Bosnian self-awareness." Did it all start with the Ottomans? With the "draft" that the Ottomans wrote or did not write? Is it, in short, Islam, impalement, and a silk cord?

How did Bosniaks come to be?

Were they created by the Islamization of the population of Bosnia? Who did that? Are they Ottomans? How? Was it voluntary? Did the inhabitants, who wanted to avoid the Ottoman levies intended for the Christian population, accept Islam and the privileges that Islam gave them?

Can the „belated" Bosniak nation identify with the whole of Bosnia?

Where did the Ottomans come from in Bosnia? What are their clues? Did the Ottomans want to impose more on Bosnia and Europe than what Bosnia and Europe could and wanted to accept? Were their means and methods from noble motives? Why didn't Europe accept them as such, if they were worthy of acceptance? Are the recurrences of Ottoman methods and actions in the Balkans recognized today?

It seems that certain influences are from the West, Njegosh, Serbia, Venice, and Austria, for a reason, distrustful of the Ottomans and that they had seen through them. This is supported by the fact that the Ottoman Empire was abolished

November 1, 1922, and the established Republic of Turkey, October 29, 1929, with Kemal Ataturk as president, after the defeat of the Ottoman Empire, in World War I by the victorious powers - the Triple Entente (Europe).

REVIEWS AND COMMENTS

ARTISTIC PHILOSOPHY

EXPRESSION OF SUBLIMATED SPIRITUALITY

Nirvana - a place of perfect peace and happiness, like heaven.[15]

We have been taught since childhood that history is the teacher of life. Society (people) needs to learn from lessons from the past to develop and progress. However, what if history loses that place in the development of a country and leaves it to a less competent discipline as a basis for educating new generations? Could this consequently lead to a misunderstanding of reality and the breaking of the connecting

---

15 Nirvana is the highest state that someone can attain, a state of enlightenment, meaning a person's desires and suffering go away.

thread of society? Or even worse - to the collapse of that society due to the wrong perception of its development by obscuring historical facts, sometimes even keeping them silent? And who, then, can answer these and similar questions?

A new book by Zeljko Vujovic with the symbolic title "Bosnia needs to be passed," deals with this very problem, illuminating it from several angles of the humanities, gathered under the auspices of the oldest science in the world, the one from which all the others developed - philosophy. Therefore, this work is a kind of compilation of history, sociology, psychology, philosophical thinking about man, autobiography, lyrical prose, and poetry. In it, the author offers an answer on a symbolic level, available to those who are ready to look at today's events without ideological obfuscation and dive into the dark realms of the self. Because spiritually we were, and we are still in Europe as much as we are not. If necessary, we often forget that the cosmos consists of an infinite number of microcosms and that the flutter of butterfly wings at one end of the world causes a storm at the other. The book is divided into three parts in which the author symbolically connects the history of Bosnian society with the fate of the individual, which inevitably brings us to the question of whether collective and personal tragedy caused by injustice can be separated. It begins with aporia (aporia: an unsolvable or difficult-to-solve problem that arises when there are two conflicting, incompatible theses about something considered) of the main character Elijah Of Thunder, who has nothing in the way visiting Vienna, Paris, or London, and yet never was in those cities. The beginning is incompatible with the first part called "Contemporary Philosophy", in which the author summarizes the history of the contemporary Bosnian struggle for statehood on the Balkan and European political stages. In epistolary form,[16] Elijah Of Thunder and the independent state of Bosnia and Herzegovina learn from each other, expanding their horizons, because Ms. NDBiH talks about tragedy, centuries of the suffering of the Bosniak people, forgotten genocides, and cries for independence, while Elijah lower historical facts available to him. Their letters also reveal the suppressed spirituality of society - which had a printed dictionary in 1631 and a grammar in 1903, ie the language - whose name is today disputed by destructive elements. That same society has its Nobel laureates and Oscar winners, and yet it is still on the margins of European spirituality. Paradoxically,

---

16   Epistolary form is polylogical writing (in which there are several characters). The reader becomes part of the character, part of the world in which it is read. It helps the reader to connect more easily with the characters.

Bosnia is the oldest organized country under that name in the Balkans and did not change it in the 19th century when the territories were named after the peoples who inhabited them, and today nationalism and the eradication of all ties between its descendants are growing in it.[17] With a sudden turn, the author moves from the collective to the personal level and talks about Elijah's fall in his microcosm - about an educated, hard-working, dedicated man and how he loses his job, on the margins of the Montenegrin social stage. Paradoxically, the social group that pushed him out of his job and left him without existence is the same social group he continues to care about refugees from war-torn Bosnia.

However, the most symbolic places in the first part are two almost Brechtian surreal plays. In them, the author reveals the course and protagonists of the process by which he is removed from the social stage (workplace). But this time he is moving from the personal to the global: Elijah Of Thunder man fueled by the spiritual values of Petar Petrovic Njegosh, Fernando Pessoa, Jesenjin, and the brilliant philosophical and artistic thoughts, acts like Josef K. – unprepared for evil, unprepared for resist, and completely surprised, even ignorant of what was happening to him, to finally discover the full weight of the philosophy of man written by dr. Scott Peck, Ph.D. Todor Baković, Todor Živaljević Velički, Sonja Tomović-Šundić and others. The source of all storms is always some kind of "drft" as an idea leading to evil: in Bosnia, in Serbia, in Montenegro, in Europe, outside of it. To be human, you must fight against nationalism, religions that bring discord, unenlightenment, darkness, evil, and hunger for power, in your environment, and for all humanity, fight with knowledge, truth, facts, and deeds. It is precisely in that place that the Anthean's complex of escape into nature develops,

---

17   Today's knowledge of the political situation in the Western Balkans during the early Middle Ages is incoherent and confusing. At that time, the South Slavs were baptized. Bosnia is mentioned, for the first time, in the middle of the 10th century in the style of "On the management of the empire, " by the Byzantine emperor Constantine Porphyrogenitus, like Serbia. Bosnia is also mentioned in the "Chronicle of Pope Dukljanin", also as an integral part of Serbia.

There are also more precise data. Described with the adjective medieval, Bosnia began to be mentioned in 958. The Serbian and Croatian principalities divided Bosnia in the 9th and 10th centuries, during the reign of Prince Časlav and King Bodin of Duklja. Bosnia became part of a single Serbian state, and in the meantime, Bosnia was ruled by Croatian King Mihailo Krešimir II. In short, at the time it was first mentioned, Bosnia was just a geographical term. The first known Bosnian ban was the Hungarian vassal Borić (1150 - 1163). 1463 - Bosnia falls, ingloriously, without a single fight under Turkish rule. That year, the Bosnian Sandzak was formed, after the execution of Stefan Tomašević.

Source: *vikipedija.org / srel / vikipedia.org / srel / Bosna_i_Hercegovina / Medieval Bosnia*

beyond the reach of the forces of evil, which, anywhere in the world, follow someone's „Draft" without choosing means of lies.[18]

Therefore, the protagonists of his plays bear such "juicy" names - from which the relationship between the authors and them is revealed: Abbot Stefan (the bearer of philosophical thought in "The Mountain Wreath", experientially says that life is a constant struggle in which one can earn an honorable name if a man fights for the general ideals of freedom and humanity), Anemic Director (weak man, incapable of life, dull, without the joys of life), but also far more direct names: Magnetic Resonant Imager, Diabetes, Depressed Optimist or KKK1, KKK2, and KKK3 in Montenegro (alluding to members of the Ku–Klux–Klan, an organization founded in 1865 that advocates white Protestant supremacy in the United States). Even the name of the main character Elijah Of Thunder is symbolic because it connects him with Elijah Thunderer - a saint who drives a car through the clouds and thus causes thunder, and who is also the patron saint of Bosnia and Herzegovina (Bishop Fr. Pavao Dragichevich asked the Holy See that Saint Elijah be celebrated as the protector of the Kingdom of Bosnia because, in addition to Catholics, he is also respected by both Orthodox and Muslims, which was approved by a document dated August 26, 1752).

The second part of the book is entitled "Contemporary Poetry"[19] in which, along with carefully selected verses, the author puts poetry on the side of spirituality. He gives it a high place by placing it between philosophy and religion, as two spiritual counterbalances (personal reflection and a complete system of moral values) that help man to know good and evil. Poetry is the cry of the human soul in a moment of unrest, whether prompted by deep sorrow or euphoric joy. Poets always point to emotion and beauty, they think with the right side of the brain and see the hidden connections between nature and man, revealing their laws. That is why the world would be an ideal place if it was the way they aspire. Indeed, poetry is a special form of spirituality that transcends all temporal and spatial boundaries. It is the source of a person's experience and starts from the personal to all people who experience similar conditions. It connects souls and gives them strength when they are most needed - when they are left alone with themselves, on the margins of the social stage. But he does so in a secretive, mysterious way, showing

---

18   What is the „draft" now in Bosnia? Is it better than the infamous „Draft" from 1844? „This is more planned" seeks a wider interest of the audience. Tear down „that" to spread „this". Who „drafts" there in Bosnia and the Microcosm? (Ž. V.)
19   This part of the book has been omitted and a special edition is foreseen.

the lust of the body as a spirit hungry for power, which always finds new victims andenjoys the human flesh it feedson.[20]

Vujović vividly shows this by commenting, giving readers comments about the experience of the poems they read. The value of poetry from the aspect of universality should be explained by the science of literature, which it does when it does not close its eyes. Just like history - when it does not turn a blind eye to certain events. The reality is often that it is easier not to know that something has happened than to face the truth. It is precisely this "squinting of science" that is the cradle of the desire to seek recognition in another world, but the question is whether it can be satisfied for non-recognition in one's environment. So you continue to heal, through poetry, the wounds that cannot be healed.

Finally, the third part of the book is autobiographical, also symbolically imbued with the covers of books received as gifts - with dedications, from which we read the history of the author's spirit, which works influenced the formation of his views and ideas as about the world, and good and evil. In the third part, the author in the form of autobiographical sketches presents memoirs from childhood and youth, memories of beautiful moments of friendship and harmony, love and dreams, revealing a personal microcosm from the time before the death of innocence, injustice, and internal struggles. As history does, he documents his life by presenting material evidence for all that is today, even his father's will. Because a man, just like the people (society), has documents that prove his integrity: birth certificate, school certificates, awards and certificates of appreciation for participating in competitions, university degree, the decision on employment, marriage certificate, certificate of residence, children's birth certificates, wills (and the state: founding act, constitution, founding acts of the ministry, laws, decisions, proclamations, etc.). The author presents documents important for his designation as a poet who sided with spirituality in the fight against evil. It is his poetic cry: *This is me, you cursed souls, naked before you with all my successes, loves, pleasures, and the cornerstone of personality. These are the roots of my canopy.*[21]

---

20 Lust is the decision to do, in our minds, what we would like to do with the body: anger, rage, madness, a strong desire to get what we achieve, to achieve by going crazy for what, an irresistible love desire, passion. Songs, in which the reviewer, recognized the description of lust, were left out to be part of some future, special edition. (Ž.V.)

21 After the evaluation of the working material for the book, which I received from Dr. Žarko Đurović, and the confirmation of that evaluation, which I received from Božana Jelušić, a professor from Budva, I chose that this third part of the book, omit and publish as a separate issue.

"Bosnia needs to be passed" by Zeljko Vujovic is a complex work from several aspects. First, its formal material consists of letters, plays, scenes, lyrical prose, essays, reflections, poetry (by the author and other poets), memoirs, historical data, photographs, comments, and newspaper articles. Thus, the author has made great strides in summarizing different types of text in one work, ranging from scientific (history, philosophy) through literary (poetry and prose) to documentary (photographs, comments, and newspaper articles). Seemingly incompatible, just like a personality composed of different emotions, memories, states, cognitions, and the environment, time, and space in which he lives, which determine his behavior. Secondly, further analysis of the text reveals the writer's *modus operandi*[22] in shaping this work and the intention to symbolically connect the individual and social learning from the past (history and psychology) to explain the role of man in social movements and laws in society and sociology), and to translate all that experience with artistic technique (literature) into a scientific thesis, for which he presents material evidence (available historical data on Wikipedia, comments, memories, and photographs-documentary).

Third, the artistic value of this book is contained in the extraordinary graded deduction, careful selection of reference texts, strong emotional images, and the construction of characters that carry the ideological basis of the work. Take, for example, the letters between Elijah Of Thunder and Mrs. NDBiH that were from the beginning coldly polite, but over time their tone changes and they become closer and more open, evoking in their form and content the correspondence of the two people who have never met, but in their letters reveal that they have many points of contact. However, the greatest value of this work is its symbolically represented idea that every man should, like a poet, touch the most hidden emotions within himself, while constantly learning and searching for the truth, no matter how painful it may be. One should fight with oneself and accept the truth and oppose evil with spirituality and reflection. In other words, every person should go through Bosnia and search for the truth about the nature of the last conflict in this country, which has four names depending on generally accepted interpretations on different sides: Civil War in BiH, Aggression in BiH, Defensive-Patriotic War, and, Homeland War. Only when a person knows all the facts and does not turn a blind eye to them, but lives and accepts them deep inside, will he understand the causes of conflicts and his real role in them. They will understand the causes and consequences, as well as the importance

22 modus operandi - way of behaving, habits, way of working, method of working or behaving. (Ž. V.)

of the unwritten "anti- draft". Because, as the author says, nationalism is the king of all evil.

It follows from all this that this philosophical work is of high artistic quality, which in content and significance can be classified as artistic philosophy, and reveals that escaping from the truth does not lead to peace, progress, development, and harmony. On the contrary, it is the source of constant conflicts in man and society. And a brake on going to Vienna, Paris or London, because only by learning and broadening our horizons do we get out of the margins of Europe.

Tamara A. Čapelj[23]

---

23 Tamara A. Čapelj works in "Planet Poetry", Sarajevo, Bosnia and Herzegovina. She graduated from the Faculty of Philosophy in Sarajevo.

"BOSNIA NEDS TO BE PASSED"
by ZELJKO VUJOVIC

This multidisciplinary philosophical and polemical work of Željko Vujović is characterized by the pluralism of methods of different scientific fields, thus opening many questions, very important for the modern society and our region.

In this part, methods from philology, history, sociology, art, and even politics are intertwined. This variety of multidisciplinary methods is sublimated and expressed in the ambiguous, almost ironic–humoristic title of the work itself, which has also become a phrase – Bosnia needs to be passed – which emphasizes the complexity of this territory, both culturally and demographically (it has always been multiethnic and multi– confessional) – and it is so complex that they should be observed, which is not at all simple.

During its history, BiH, or some parts of it belonged to different states and were under different state systems (independent, autonomous, then under Turkish rule, then under Austro-Hungarian, then within different variants of Yugoslavia, and since 1993. year again as independent and autonomous). These changes also affected its population, whose composition could not be permanent due to all that, disrupted by various types of migration, both to its territory and from it.

When one part of it became an independent state at the beginning of the 1990s, it was necessary to build an identity. Of course, the question of language was one of the first to arise. Until then, the Serbo–Croatian language was used and spoken in this territory. With recognized independence, there is a need to have their language, which is diachronic,24 historically based. This is the right of every nation to be

---

24   diachrony - diversity, the occurrence of some phenomena at different times. An account of the development of a language in different periods.

respected, but the facts must not be falsified, relativized, and misused for that purpose, as doesthe character from this part of the NDBiH, who is the paradigm of all relations, the confusion of the „aporias of Elijah Of Thunder" from this work, to whom and whose people are accused of various crimes including those from the distant past.

The greatest confusions and aporias currently in the social sciences and humanities in this area are caused by (un) conscious anachronisms,[25] mostly out of a desire for national continuity, and the diachronic perspective is selectively taken into account – if it is in favor of building that continuity, the facts stand out, otherwise, they are not mentioned, some are even falsified.

NDBiH will point out:

"That the first dictionary of the Bosnian language was published in 1631, about 180 years before the first Serbian dictionary, and 200 years before the first Croatian dictionary?" Continuing further, the NDBiH, based on rather chronologically continuous historical facts, continues its argumentation about language:

"Language is the basic determinant of man. Who speaks whose language? Bosnian grammar was written before Vuk Karadzic' s grammar. Bosnian is not an artificial language."

From which the artificial and aggressive deduction, within which some facts are silenced and others are overemphasized, implied how:

"The Bosnian language has greater historical justifications than the Serbian language."

Respecting the right of each people to its language, considering the above arguments, it is noted:

1. The Bosnian–Turkish dictionary, by Muhammed Hevai Uskufi, was published in 1631.

This argument and confirmation from the first half of the 17th century are interpreted anachronistically – by the criteria of modern aspects. The concept of nation and national consciousness and language, in the modern sense, was constituted at the beginning and middle

---

25 anachronism - an error in calculating the date, event, what is contrary to chronology, temporal disorder, imperfection; neglect of what suits the spirit and circumstances of the time, e.g. cannons in the Battle of Kosovo, Caesar in a car, etc.; obsolescence, backwardness, obsolescence, maintenance of outdated and surviving conceptions.

of the 19th century. This Dictionary was written and published for administrative and economic practical needs, to make it easier for the population from the territory of BiH, which was multiethnic at the time, to reach an agreement with the Turks.

Therefore, this dictionary does not reflect the state and vocabulary of a language but is specialized, and bilingual for practical use and communication. The adjective "Bosnian" in the title meant more territory than the national–linguistic determinant of the time.

2. It is quite clear in science: that the basis for the standard Serbian and Croatian languages are the East Herzegovinian dialects, ie the East Herzegovinian dialect of the Bosnian language.

This second argument is very bold but false and inaccurate. Vuk Stefanović Karadžić took the East Herzegovinian dialect as the basis of the literary language, as the most developed language in that period, and he knew it best. Speaking about the language of this dialect, Vuk was unequivocal in the Preface to the first edition of the Serbian Dictionary, where he pointed out, among other things: „He published his grammar for these very reasons, as a small reputation for how Serbs use names and their conjugate verbs. The dictionary is published so that writers can see how people speak.

All the words in the dictionary exist in the people; some words are in the people and not in the dictionary because he has not heard them and does not know about them.

Even if not all Serbian words have been collected ,at least the foundation has been laid to gather them (as much as possible in a living language)'.

Explains the way Serbian words are interpreted in Latin and German words and accepts the possibility of some translation errors.

To better explain some words (their origin and use), he described some customs and added short stories…"

He clearly and unequivocally pointed out that it was the Serbian language, which the Serbs used in the first decades of the 19th century and which was fairly standardized with his editions of „Dictionary" and „Grammar" and after the Vienna Agreement (1850) became officially literary claims that this dialect belongs to any other language are completely unfounded and inaccurate.

So, as for the basis, that is, the East Herzegovinian dialect, which was established by the middle of the 19th century, as Vuk Stefanović

Karadžić pointed out in his works, belongs to the Serbian language corpus.

3. In the Library of the Matica Srpska in Novi Sad, there is not only an edition of the Grammar of the Bosnian language from 1890 but also from 1898 and 1903 - which is true, but it is a short period because in 1907 it was a new protector, for Bosnia and Herzegovina, was Burian, who issued the order on October 4, 1907. important for the further strengthening of language flows in Bosnia and Herzegovina, in which, among other things, it reads: The country's government hereby intends to completely abandon the use of the language of these countries as Bosnian in all official traffic and in all documents of the country's government, and that, in favor of the country's language, without exception has a valid Serbo–Croatian language. How could they ban what does not exist?

In this short period, which lasted the longest from 1890–to 1910, there is an increased linguistic and national consciousness in BiH, which is confirmed by the editions of these Grammars, but already in 1910, the Serbo-Croatian language was used and served in BiH, from then until 1993, when it was necessary to build a new national-linguistic consciousness, and whether this could be done based on falsification of facts (claims that a certain dialect belongs to another language "more" than that for which there is explicit confirmation); anachronistic interpretation of facts (facts from the 17th century are interpreted according to modern standards, which as such did not even exist at that

time); let it remain open, while the truth and explicit evidence, which have already been mentioned in this text, must not be silenced.

The situation regarding the so–called Bosnian language, Dr. Rada Stijović expressed it best: "The author of these lines believes that the term Bosnian language is unacceptable not only for linguistic reasons but also because it suggests that it is spoken by all inhabitants of Bosnia and Herzegovina, and ultimately that all inhabitants of BiH are one – the Bosnian nation. That this is not just a calculation is shown by the statement of the publisher of the mentioned Uskufi's dictionary, who said at the promotion in Zagreb that the dictionary was intended for Bosniaks of all three religions, who spoke one language – Bosnian, and which has been confirmed since Kulin's charter. True, the terms Bosniak and bosniak do not differ much – they suggest that Bosniaks are the only authentic people in Bosnia and that the other two are not. However, the terms have been accepted and there is nothing more to discuss them.

Just as today's Bosniaks and other peoples have been given the right to name a common literary language (whose source is predominantly Serbian), so we must not take that right away from those who in the past have declared themselves to write in Serbian, or what is written in the Serbian. Therefore, care must be taken to ensure that linguistic monuments such as Kulin's Charter or Miroslav's Gospel and the works of Selimović, Kulenović, and Andrić are studied in schools in Serbia as part of the Serbian linguistic and cultural heritage.

Such attitudes are not a challenge to the right of others to cultural identity, but the preservation of one's cultural heritage and one's own identity.[26]

This text sheds light on the "aporias of Elijah Of Thunder" from this work by Zeljko Vujovic, with whom he should "pass Bosnia", this complex, modern, expressed through the character of NDBiH, while preserving good, clearly differentiating evil, and then be that spark, she the light that brings light, illuminates and illuminates the unexplained, which Zeljko Vujović initiated with this work, and clarified to the wise and attentive reader.

I am sure that you will be happy to read - because "Bosnia needs to be passed" - everyone will find some reasons for that, and that is the wealth, beauty and charm.

Marina Đenedić[27]

---

26   Dr. Rada Stijović, KulinBan has written Cyrillic, „Politika", Sep. 19.2015
27   Marina Đenadić works at the Belgrade City Library. She graduated from the Faculty of Philology, University of Belgrade.

EVALUATION

Dear Željko,

I was happy to read your working material for the book. I intentionally haven't read the reviews yet, so as not to affect me. While reading the book, I became convinced of what I knew about you, that you are an exceptional intellectual and that you carry all the peculiarities that makeup one of your units of general education!

Your versatility, which is indisputable in everything you have participated in and succeeded in, in my and general opinion, has had a very negative effect on the destination and style that you are constantly guided by in this book.

I don't know how to classify a book in any genre. Sometimes it seems to be a short story, sometimes a novel, sometimes an autobiographical work...? The book is full of variety and unusualness, as well as some curiosity, supported by the participants, who give emotional but irrelevant facts. That would significantly affect the controversy about the intention of such communication and its goal!?

I think that in this controversy between Mrs. NDBiH and Elijah Of Thunder, we should avoid the benevolence and emphasis on her personal experience, which happened in Bosnia, as the fault of Serbian nationalism, Njegosh, Serbian Orthodox Church, Chetniks, Ustashas, the oldest Bosnian language and the like.!? With the attitude of Elijah Of Thunder, which is based more on courtesy and indulgence in mutual communications, you reduce the importance of this literary work. I think so! Of course, we can discuss that when we see each other soon in Podgorica. The autobiographical part of this work, which I like, does not, again, in my opinion, disagree with the given topic.[28]

---

28 This is well said. Even great! What do excerpts from my autobiography, torn from oblivion, have to do with the tragedy, centuries of the suffering of the Bosniak people, the forgotten genocides, and the cry for independence, with some Elijah Of Thunder and the Unfortunate Refugee Spy from Bosnia, from Sarajevo, doing

Historical records and citations of footnotes also point to scientific work, not a novel or anything like that.

I appreciate your philosophical thoughts and some conclusions, Dostoevsky's ideas, but, very often, but?!

I also appreciate the beautiful writing, general education, and communication of the NDBiH lady in question, from Bosnia, but not her conclusions and view of the situation on the general issue. I understand the indignation and hatred of all the people who survived the war in the former Yugoslavia. Bosnia needs to be passed or told one time, seeing the participants in the war and observers from a distance is difficult to fit, reconcile and describe in literature. I know that was not the goal, but it is the conclusion of the reader.

I am sure that one should consult well with another experienced writer, who would give instructions and solve the flow of writing. Perhaps he would divide the book into two parts: Bosnia needs to be passed and My biography - torn from oblivion.

It's late, it's two o'clock in the morning, and I'm writing to you. I would very much like to be able to give good advice, but it requires more consultation than my assessment.

Žarko Đurović[29]

---

the dirthy work for an Anemic Director?? In what way does the modern lady of the NDBiH return her gratitude for taking care of the poor, unfortunate, escaped Spies from Bosnia, showing that books are published in Bosnia and Herzegovina as well ? I will omit the autobiographical part for a special publication. (Ž. V.) An era that began with the fall of the Berlin Wall and socialism, and continued with the rise of the Mexican Wall and neoliberal capitalism, is coming to an end. In Podgorica, those for whom the street is the only free institution shout: "Keep the thief!" What are the "Drafts" of the Federation of BiH, the Microcosm, and Balcans today? Who "draws" it there? How much money should be paid, in Microcosm, to "draft?" (Ž. V.)

29   Žarko Đurović is a doctor in the field of social sciences and humanities. Lives in Belgrade. In a private conversation, he told me that he would not write those things about the "Microcosm" that I wrote down. He told me about Miško: „He did something worthwhile, but it was worthwhile for the Hospital. Not to mention hemodialysis machines. Not even a cobalt bomb."

WE AND EUROPE 2018: The Western Balkans and the European Union until something new happens ...

Izvor: Vikipedija, Istorija Evropske Unije

There are similarities between Switzerland and the Western Balkans. The only difference is that Switzerland is Switzerland, and the Western Balkans is the Western Balkans.

CORRESPONDENCE

with a legal entity registered to perform publishing activities in the Federation of Bosnia and Herzegovina

Date 24.02.2019. 16:10, Damir Uzunović[30] Wrote:

Dear Željko,

I really thought I answered you earlier, because very soon after sending the text by transfer, I had a clear position, so I apologize for the omission, but I will do it now. The text is really interesting, but it remains unclear why and for whom you are writing it, whether you are defending Bosnia or someone else. There is a lot of unconvincingness and I think that the text was created out of entertainment and to entertain the lazy population and not to teach or defend the one whose maneuvering possibilities for defense have been drastically reduced. As an editor and then as a publisher, I have to tell you that the text, in my opinion, would not meet the wider interest of the audience, which is crucial, so unfortunately I say that we are not interested in publishing, which does not mean you can not offer it to someone else. to the publisher.

With respect,

Damir Uzunović, director and editor

---

30   Damir Uzunović is the owner of the Buy book publishing house from Sarajevo and a member of the Association of Publishers of Bosnia and Herzegovina.

Date 26.02.2019. 09:44, Željko Vujović wrote:

Dear Damir,

I'm sorry that you didn't find interest in publishing my book, that is, to publish it together. I wish it was.

Why and for whom am I writing? For readers.

Am I defending Bosnia or someone else? I am defending Bosnia, but that was not said too pretentiously by me! How can I defend Bosnia and why should I defend it? Who else should I defend? Who is the one whose maneuverability has been drastically reduced, so that I can teach and defend him? Who did it and why? What is the denied maneuverability?

Why didn't you state, specifically, what these uncertainties are, so that they can be removed, if necessary?

This is how you were left unsaid and "short-sleeved".

In any case, I express my sincere respect to you, your editors, Kristina Ljevak and Ida Hamidović. I wish you success in life and work.

With respect, Zeljko Vujovic

APPENDIX

I'm giving up. I will no longer defend Bosnia. I am defending Portugal. I want to suffer because Bosnia is not interested in one of the most difficult topics in our modern history. I want to suffer because I am unconvincing, unlike Bosnia, which is convincing. I want to suffer because it is not crucial for me as it is crucial for Damir Uzunović. I want to suffer because I did not appear at the 63rd International Book Fair in Belgrade, unlike Damir, and because I learned that the Federation of Bosnia and Herzegovina exists and that books are still published there. I want to suffer because the Federation of BiH has everything, only books are missing. This was stated by Damir in an interview he gave to Sarajevo's Oslobodjenje at the 63rd Belgrade Book Fair, where he attended the largest book market in the Balkans. He stated that in the capacity of a representative publisher from BiH.

Damir's letter is dated February 24, 2019. His statement in the same interview, that the Federation of BiH is "ready for any kind of cooperation with authors, booksellers, literary critics from Belgrade and the surrounding area, can be highlighted and viewed from another angle." It is important that the Federation lists every book that enters it, and charges a fee for each one. In that interview, at the 63rd Book Fair in Belgrade, Damir did not talk about "someone whose maneuvering abilities for defense have been drastically reduced". Who is that? He talked about marketing, selling, and reading books. He said, explicitly, clearly, and unequivocally, "that the Federation of BiH has everything, only its books are missing."

REGISTER OF PERSONAL NAMES[31]

REFERENCES

1. Karl R. Popper, "Open Society and Its Enemies", Belgrade Publishing Institute 1993.
2. "Southeast Europe 1918 - 1995", International Scientific Conference, Zadar 1995.
3. Petar II Petrović Njegoš, "Gorski vijenac", Unirex - Nikšić, Narodno delo - Belgrade
4. Petar II Petrovic Njegos, "Luca mikrokozma", Unirex - Niksic, Narodno - Delo, Belgrade
5. Dr. Scott Peck, "People of Lies", IP WORLDS / NOVI SAD, 1995.
6. Dr. Todor Baković, "The sky is opening", Pobjeda, Podgorica, 2007.
7. Fernando Pessoa, "Book of Troubles", Dereta, Belgrade, 2017.
8. Todor Živaljević Velički, "Metoh i Ja", „
9. Hamdija Šarkinović, "Organization of the Turkish Government in Montenegro", Matica crnogorska, 2013.
10. Petar Korunić, "Jugoslovenska ideja / Južnoslovenska ideja", original scientific paper, 10. March 2009, capnia slavonica 9 (2009) 471- 518
11. Diwan – the magazine of modern Bosniak thougdarwinawin- magazine. com, March 2, 2018.
12. http://www.pornani.sk/img/detail/4548/cierna-hora-   durmitor-s-morem-dolomity-balkanu-np-durmitor-s- morem_13247.jpg
13. http://www.facebook.com/sokantna.istina (Shocking historical truth)
14. https://www.facebook.com/medinadzanbegovicmohamed/posts/102022776462682827, Facebook, Dec 11, 2014.
15. http://www.republica.co.rs/548-549/21Html
- Sonja Biserko, Latinka Perović, "Documents on the Crimes of Bosnian Serbs", Minutes from the Assembly of the Republika Srpska (1991-1996)
- Robert Donis, "Every Serb has a gun and a ticket" - From the Assembly of Republika Srpska 1991-1996.
16. http://www.facebook.com/mirjana.kuljak
17. Wikipedia.org/srel/Bosna_i_Hercegovina/Srednjevjekovna_Bo sna
18. Wikipedia, History of the European Union

APSTRAKT

Pojedinci, zajednice, narodi, nacije, države, društvo na prostoru Zapadnog Balkana. Njihovi međusobni odnosi i uti-caji, kao i odnosi sa susjednim društvima i Evropom u cje- lini. Pregled i promišljanje o istorijskim sukobima, koji su se dešavali na Zapadnom Balkanu i odnos i uticaj Evrope prema tim sukobima. Odraz tih ratova na živote pojedinaca,države i čitavog društva na Zapadnom Balkanu. Podsticanje na razmišljanje postavljanjem pitanja. Ko od koga treba da uči? Zapadni Balkan od Evrope ili Evropa od Zapadnog Bal-kana?

U knjizi su opisane stvarne ličnosti i stvarni događaji. Dat je registar ličnih imena, koja su poslužila kao inspiracijaza pisanje knjige, s tim da je nekim od tih imena dato lite- rarno, simboličko ime s ciljem da knjiga dobije beletristički karakter. Druga imena su ostavljena u originalu.

Rijeka Bosna i Vrelo Bosne su nepresušni izvor života u centru Zapadnog Balkana… svijet i biser… blago u koje treba da zaronimo…

ABSTRACT

Individuals, communities, peoples, nations, states, and society in the Western Balkans. Their mutual relations and influences, as well as relations with neighboring societies and Europe as a whole. An overview and reflection on historical conflicts that took place in the Western Balkans and the relationship and influence of Europe on these conflicts. The impact of these wars on the lives of individuals, the states, and the entire society in the Western Balkans. Stimulating thinking by asking questions. Who should learn from whom? Western Balkans from Europe or Europe from the Western Balkans?

The book describes the real personality and actual events.

A register of personal names is provided. It served as inspiration for writing the book. Some of these names were given a literary, symbolic name to get the book a literary character. Other names were left in the original.

The river Bosnia and the Source of river Bosnia are a source of life that does not dry up in the center of the Western Balkans

… a world and a pearl… a treasure that we need to dive into…

РЕЗЮМЕ

Лица, общины, народы, нации, гостударства, обще- ство на Западных Балканах. Их взаимоотношения и влияния, а также отношения с соседними обществами и Европой в це- лом. Обзор и отражение исторических конфликтов, которые имели место на Западных Балка нах, а также отношения и влияние Европы на эти конфликты. Отражение этих войн о жизни отдельных людей, государства и всего общества на Западных Балканах. Поощряйте мышление, задавая вопросы. Кому нужно учиться? Западные Балканы из Европы или Европы с Западных Балкан?

В книге описываются реальные личности и реаль- ные события. Дается реестр личных имен, который по- служил источником вдохновения для написания книги, причем некоторые из этих имен получили литературное символическое имя, чтобы получить литературный ха- рактер книги. Остальные имена остаются в оригинале.

Река Босна и Источник реки Боснии являются источ- ником жизни, которие не высыкают, в центре Западных Балканах … мир и жемжучный … богатство, которое нам ну- жно погрузиться …

RÉSUMÉ

Individus, communautés, peuples, nations, États, soci été des Balkans occidentaux. Leurs relations et influences mutuelles, ainsi que leurs relations avec les sociétés voisines et avec l'Europe dans son ensemble. Bilan et réflexion sur les conflits historiques survenus dans les Balkans occidentaux et sur les relations et l'influence de l'Europe contre ces conflits. Réflexion de ces guerres sur la vie des individus, de l'État et de la société tout entière dans les Balkans occidentaux. Encouragez la réflexion en posant des questions. Qui a besoin d'apprendre? Balkans occidentaux d'Europe ou d'Europe des Balkans occidentaux?

Le livre décrit la personnalité réelle et les événements réels. Un registre de noms de personnes est donné, qui a servi d'in- spiration à la rédaction d'un livre. Certains de ces noms se sont vus attribuer un nom littéraire et symbolique afin d'obtenir le caractère littéraire du livre. Les autres noms sont laissés dans l'original.

Rivière Bosna et la ource de la rivièra Bosna son tune source de vie indestructible au centre des Balkans occiden taux

… monde et perle … le trésor dans leqel nouns devrions prolonger…

Cataloging in the National Library of Montenegro in the Montenegrin language

CIP - Katalogizacija u publikaciji Nacionalna biblioteka Crne Gore, Cetinje

94(497.6)
821.163.4-94
Napomene: slika autora: str. 127, bilješke uz tekst, bibliografija: str. 121, registar, rezimei na više jezika.

ISBN 978-9940-9836-3-5

a)   Bosna
b)   Društveno-političke prilike

NOTE ON THE AUTHOR

![photograph]

Željko Vujović on one of his tasks.

www.ingramcontent.com/pod-product-compliance
Lightning Source LLC
Chambersburg PA
CBHW051211120626
46547CB00013B/1301